LEARN HOW TO USE MS EXCEL IN 2023

WITH NEW VERSION OF EXCEL

PREPARED BY
REAGAN KUNGU FRANCIS (B.E)

PREFACE

In this course you will learn how to get started with excel and how to process data in the excel. Excel program is important in our society today because it help to manage and manipulate data easily and save time which is lost do to many mistakes made during the processing of the data manually. So, it is important to know excel in detail, after you finish to read you will understand why need this course.

Other books in this series which you can buy and read are the following:

Book 1: Learn How to Use Computer (New Versions of Windows)

Book 2: Learn How to Use Microsoft Word in 2023

Book 3: Learn How to Use Microsoft Excel in 2023

Book 4: Learn How to Use Microsoft PowerPoint in 2023

Book 5: Learn How to Use Microsoft Publisher in 2023

You can contact me if you have any suggestion about this book by the following contact.

Email info: francisreagan88@gmail.com

TABLE OF CONTENTS

PART ONE

GET STARTED WITH MICROSOFT EXCEL

1.1. INTRODUCTION TO MS EXCEL

What is the Spreadsheet or Excel

Excel is all about numbers! There's almost no limit to what you can do with numbers in Excel, including sorting, advanced calculations, and graphing. In addition, Excels formatting options mean that whatever you do with your numbers, the result will always look professional!

Data files created with Excel are called workbooks (in the same way as Word files are called documents). But where Word starts up with a single blank page, Excel files by default contain three blank worksheets. This gives you the flexibility to store related data in different locations within the same file. More worksheets can be added, and others deleted, as required.

You'll often hear Excel files referred to as spreadsheets. This is a generic term, which sometimes means a workbook (file) and sometimes means a worksheet (a page within the file).

Why do I need a Spreadsheet?

There are many reasons why you might need a spreadsheet. Here are few different scenarios:

Scenario 1 - Personal Investments

You have bought shares in a few different companies and want to keep track of how well, or badly, they are doing. You could enter these values in a spreadsheet:
My Share: Share1
Price Paid: 0.25
Number Held: 1000
Total Cost: £250
Value Now: 0.35
Worth Now: £350
Profit/Loss: +£100
The spreadsheet would do all the sums for you. All you must do is enter the correct formulas. In the spreadsheet above, if we changed the number in the "Value Now" box, the "Worth Now" box and the "Profit/Loss" box will automatically be updated. That way you could see briefly how well your shares are doing.

Scenario 2 - Personal Finances

We only have a limited amount of money coming into the house each month. The problem is that money seems to be disappearing fast. If would be nice if we could keep track of where it's all going. A spreadsheet could help us. We could enter the data like this:
Monthly Income: £1500
Gas: 25
Electricity: 20
Phone: 35
HP: 250
Food: 350
Mortgage: 425

Car: 130
Total: £1235
Leftover: £265

Of course, we could do all that on a piece of paper. But entering the data into a spreadsheet gives us better control. We could change one value, that massive food bill, and see how much we had left over if we didn't spend so much money on food. Once the formulas are entered, the other figures would be updated automatically.

So, there we have two simple scenarios where a spreadsheet might come in handy. Of course, they can be used, and often are, in a business situation. If you want to keep track of things like stock and profit margins, then spreadsheets are very useful indeed. In fact, spreadsheets are useful in a wide range of situations, both business and non-business.

1.2 LAUNCHING AND EXPLORING EXCEL

For Windows 8/10 users

1. Go to the Start Button on the Desktop and press ALL apps
.

2. Then click on Excel.

3. This opens the Excel program

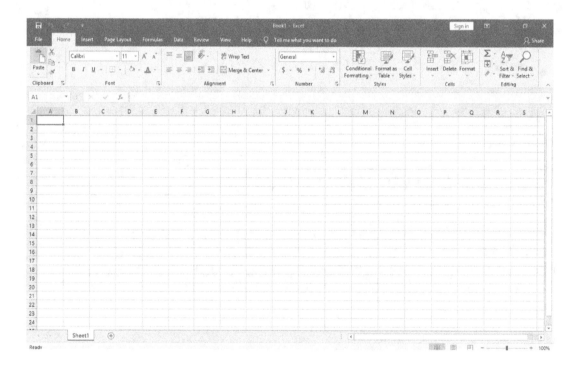

Identifying the items on the Excel program screen:

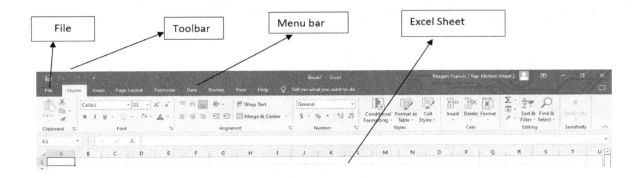

Menu bar:

1. Menu bar contains all the operators which the user wishes to perform on their Data.
2. By clicking on each tab user and view the operator. Example: By clicking on Home tab user can see the operators which allow changing the Font type, size, and color.

Toolbars:

1. A wide variety of toolbars displaying buttons which make editing quicker and easier are available.
2. Usually Toolbars have only three options: Save, Undo and Redo. Users have an option of adding any tool they wish to have in Toolbar by simply Customizing the Toolbar.

Customizing Toolbars:

1. By clicking on the small down arrow present beside Toolbar users can Customize Toolbar.
2. From the available options, user can select any option by clicking on them.

The File tab.

In the top left of the Ribbon in Excel there's a File. This one:

Click this, and you'll see all the file operations: New, Open, Save, Exit, etc.

Quick Access

The small discrete toolbar "Quick Access", where with a single click you can save, undo, etc., is located just to the right of the File Button. "Quick Access" can be customized so that you can choose the features that suit you best. You do this by right-clicking on a button and choosing Customize Quick Access Toolbar. Alternatively, you can click the small arrow to the right of the toolbar, which enables you to quickly select and deselect various features.

The Workspace

The workspace is located underneath the Ribbon, and this is where you have your spreadsheet. The spreadsheet is a huge table with "columns" and "rows". The columns are named with letters in the "column headings", and the rows are labeled with row numbers in the "row headings." By clicking on a column heading, you can select the cells in the whole column, and the same is true if you click on a row heading. The "Corner "is in the top left corner of the worksheet. By clicking on the corner, you can select all the cells in the entire worksheet. The cells are the basic elements of the worksheet; this is where we type in our data and formulas. Wherever a row and a column meet, we have a "cell". Each cell in the worksheet has a unique name. For example, the cell located where column C and row 4 meet is called "C4". A cell can contain numbers, words, and formulas. Formulas are kinds of commands that you type into a cell, which make the cell display the result of a calculation.

Sheet Tabs

The "Sheet Tabs" are located just below the worksheet, on the left side. This is because you can work with multiple worksheets at once. **An Excel file** is therefore also called a" Workbook", because it is like a folder containing several spreadsheets.

The Sheet Tabs are by default named "Sheet1", "Sheet2" etc., but you can give them more meaningful names yourself. You can also delete and add Sheet Tabs, and thus spreadsheets. If you right-click on one of the Sheet Tabs, a menu pops up giving you the opportunity to do various things.
You can add, delete, and copy Sheet Tabs, and thus the spreadsheets they represent. You can also change the order of the Tabs and give each Tab its own color, which can facilitate the overview.

Display Buttons

You can use the display buttons to adjust the way you view the spreadsheet. When you start a new spreadsheet, it is displayed in "Normal View", but you can also view it as a "Page Impression", which is somewhat like the way it would look if you were to print the sheet.
"Show page breaks" is another option, where you can view and adjust the page breaks in the print-out.

Finally, there is the zoom function, which allows you to enlarge or reduce the view of the sheet. The zoom function does not affect how the spreadsheet appears on a print-out. The zoom function is easy to use, but a better way in my opinion is to hold down the CTRL key on your keyboard while scrolling up and down with the scroll wheel on your mouse. Of course, this requires that you have a mouse with a scroll wheel.

1.3 START A NEW SPREADSHEET

When Excel starts up, the program will display a new, blank workbook. This is fine, but you do not always have to build everything up from scratch. Alternatively, you can start a new spreadsheet manually, using various templates.

1. Click on the File tab in the top left corner of the screen.
2. Click on New. You will now choose which template you want to use.

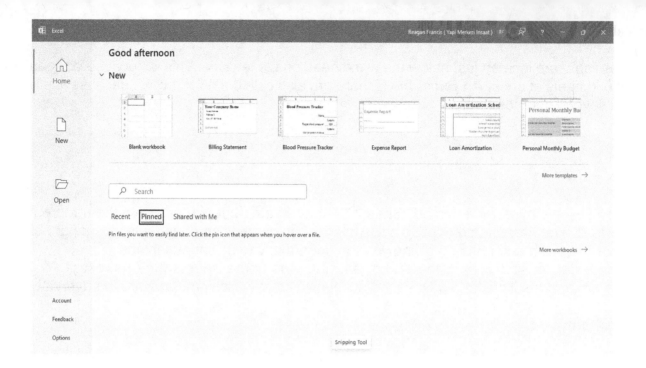

Templates for invoicing budgeting and even monitoring of blood pressure have already been installed. If you do not think the preinstalled templates are enough, it is possible to download many more via the search bar.

Navigating the spreadsheet

You can use both mouse and keyboard to navigate the worksheet, but I recommend that you practice using the keyboard. It is a faster and economically better solution.
You'll need to move things around a lot in the spreadsheet, and if you always use the mouse, you could easily develop a "mouse-arm."

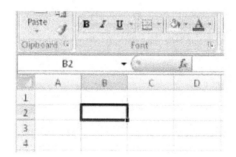

Using the keyboard to move around has other advantages which I shall return to later. There is always one, and only one, active cell in the spreadsheet. It is identified by a thick black border all around it called the "cell pointer". You can choose a second active cell using the arrow keys or the mouse. Try pressing lightly on the arrow keys on the keyboard to move the cursor.

Navigating Large Spreadsheets

When you navigate large spreadsheets, it becomes difficult to use the mouse. You can move quickly to specific locations in a spreadsheet using the keyboard. If you press down the CTRL key and press the HOME key on the keyboard, the cursor moves to cell A1. If you hold down the CTRL key and use the arrow keys, you can skip to "where something is happening, for example, be the outer edge of a table. If you have a table with 1000 rows and 50 columns in your spreadsheet, pressing the down arrow while you press down the CTRL key will take you to the last row of the table. Similarly, the up arrow will take you to the top. The principle is the same for moving right and left. This can also be used for selection of cells. If, in addition to pressing down the CTRL key, press downs the Shift key as well, the cells will be selected.

Cell Pointer and Auto Fill

If you take a close look at the cell pointer, you'll notice a small black square in the lower right corner of the cursor.
This is the location of a feature with the awkward name "Auto Fill". Auto Fill can be used via the mouse if you need to quickly copy some cells. When you point to the little black square with the mouse the mouse cursor changes to a small black cross. Keep the left mouse button down and move the mouse until you have marked some cells, then release the mouse button again. Several things can happen when you do this. Either a simple copying of content from the active cell will take place or a "series" will be introduced. If, for example, you typed "Monday" in the active cell and used Auto Fill to copy it, the subsequent cells will read "Tuesday", "Wednesday", etc. This is one kind of series. Excel has several predefined ranges for weekdays and months. You can also create your own series, and we will come back to that later in the book.

Writing in the Cells

Try typing some numbers and text in different cells. When you finish typing something into a cell, press the ENTER key on the keyboard. The cell below the cell you just typed in will become the active cell.
Note also that if you write text in a cell, the text will be aligned to the left. If you type in numbers, the figure will be adjusted to the right. If you want to change something in a cell, you can double-click on it, which enables you to change the content. If it is the active cell you want to change, you can also press F2 on your keyboard If you merely wish to add something new you just double-click on the active cell.

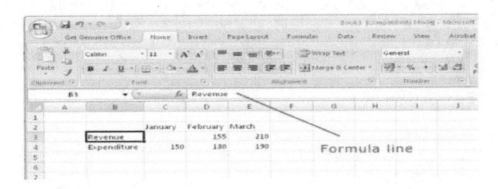

Also note the "Formula Bar", as shown in Figure 11. It is currently showing what you type into the cells and may not seem especially important right now. But later, when you use formulas in some of the cells, the Formula Bar will show what kind of formula that is used in the active cell, while the active cell displays the result.

Adaptation of Cell Size

The cells are the same from the start, but this can be changed. You can change the cell size by changing the row height and column width.

Try moving your mouse over the column headers (A, B, C, etc.). You will notice that the mouse cursor changes when it approaches a new column. When it does, you can press the left mouse button down while moving the mouse to adjust column width. The same method can be used to change the row height. Instead of clicking and dragging with your mouse, you can double-click it. This will adjust the column width so that it is just wide enough to show the largest cell in the column. You can experiment with this yourself. This method can also be used to adjust the row height.

Selecting Cells

To select a single cell, just move the cell pointer to it so that it becomes the active cell. If you want to select multiple cells, there are two ways to do it.
1. Point to a cell with the mouse, press the left mouse button down and drag the mouse, by which an area will be selected. Release the left mouse button when you have selected the area you wanted. The cell you clicked on first will be the active cell.
2. Move the cursor to the corner of the area you want to select. Hold down the Shift key on your keyboard and press the arrow keys. If you hold down the Shift the selection will be adjusted. Release the Shift key when you are done selecting.

Compound Selection

You can also select multiple independent fields at once. Here you will have to use both mouse and keyboard simultaneously. You must hold down the CTRL key on your keyboard, and then select the desired fields with the mouse. Experiment a little with it yourself.

Navigating Inside a Selection

If you have selected an area and then press one of the arrow keys on the keyboard, the selection will disappear. That is not always what we want, so instead, use the TAB key and ENTER key on your keyboard to move to the right and downward respectively. You can use the same keys to move left and upwards by pressing down the SHIFT key simultaneously.

1.4 WIDEN AN EXCEL COLUMN

To widen a column, do the following:

*   Move your mouse pointer up to the letter A

*   The pointer will be in the shape of a white cross, as in the next image.

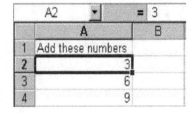

- Now move your mouse pointer, the white cross, to the line in between the A and the B

- The mouse pointer will change shape again.

- The mouse pointer will be in the shape of a black cross with arrowheads, like the one in the image below.

- When you mouse pointer changes shape, hold down your left mouse button.

- Keep it held down and drag your mouse to the right.

- Let go of the mouse button when you are satisfied with the width of your column.

Widening an Excel column,   The Result

You can widen a row in the same way.
We'll now see how to center those numbers in their cells, and format that text a little.

1.5. FORMATTING CELLS

Centering text in a cell comes under the heading of formatting. Things like making the text bold, changing the font, and adding some color also come under formatting. There is a menu in excel devoted to the subject - the format menu. Let's start with centering the data in the cells.
Before you can Format any cell data, you must "tell" Excel which cells you want to change. You do this by highlighting the cells. To highlight cells, do the following:

- Position your mouse pointer over cell A1.

- Make sure the pointer is in the shape of a thick white cross.

- Hold down your left mouse button.

- Keep the left mouse button held and drag downwards.

- Let go of the left mouse button when all four cells are highlighted.

- Your spreadsheet will look like the one below.

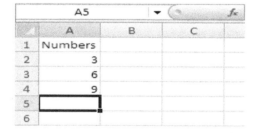

As you can see, the cells A1, A2, A3, and A4 are a different color to the other cells, which are white. Our four cells also have the darker border around them. This is because they are highlighted. Once cells have been highlighted, you can do something with them. We'll format the cells we've highlighted.

1.6. HOW TO ENTER TEXT AND NUMBERS IN A CELL

To make a start, we'll create this simple spreadsheet:

All we're going to be doing here is entering some text and some numbers. We're not adding anything up yet.

Before you tackle this first exercise, though, you may want to take note of the Undo feature just in case you make a mistake. The Undo option is the left curved arrow, right at the top of your screen.

Click the left curved arrow to Undo something and click the right curved arrow to redo it. The Undo arrow also has a dropdown box. Click the small arrow next to Undo to see the following:

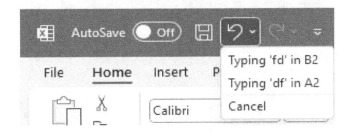

This list is for multiple Undo's. Move your mouse down the list and click to undo several steps at once. But back to the spreadsheet.
Click inside of cell A1 on your spreadsheet, and do the following:

- Type the word "Numbers" (with no quotation marks)

- Hit the Enter key on your keyboard.

- The active cell will move down one, to cell A2.

- Type the number 3, and again hit the Enter key on your keyboard.

- The active cell will move down one, to cell A3.

- Now put the number 6 into cell A3, and the number 9 in cell A4.

- After you have typed the number 9, and hit the Enter key, you should see that cell A5 is now the active cell.

You should now have a spreadsheet that looks like ours above.
The text we entered in cell A1 is known as a Heading. It's there just to tell you what the numbers mean.

1.7 HOW TO EDIT TEXT IN A CELL

In the previous part, you created a simple Excel spreadsheet. You'll now learn how to edit text in a cell.
To change the text in cell A1, you can just click inside of the cell and start typing. Anything you had their previously would be erased. But if you just want to edit the text (if you've made a spelling mistake, for example), then this is no good. If you want to keep most of the text, and just make minor changes, then you need to do something else.
In the image below, you can see what's known as the Formula Bar. The Formula Bar is like a long textbox that you can click inside and start typing. Here's what it looks like in Excel:

A5			f_x	
A	B	C	Formula Bar	E
1 Numbers				
2	3			
3	6			
4	9			
5				
6				

To edit a Cell in Excel, first click inside the cell you want to edit (A1 for us). Then click inside the formula bar. Notice where your cursor is now:

A1	▼	X ✓ f_x	Numbers

	A	B	C	D	E
1	Numbers				
2	3				
3	6				
4	9				
5					

The image above shows that the cell A1 is active, but the cursor is inside of the formula bar.
With the cursor in the Formula Bar, try changing the text "Numbers" to "Add these Numbers". Press the Enter key when you've made the changes. Your spreadsheet should look like ours below:

A2	▼	f_x	3

	A	B	C	D
1	Add these Numbers			
2	3			
3	6			
4	9			
5				

Notice that the active cell is now A2, and that the Formula Bar has a 3 in it.
However, there's a problem. There's not enough room in cell A1 for our new text. Part of it seems to be in the B column.
The solution is to widen the whole of Column A. Try this:

➔ Move your mouse up to the start of the A Column
➔ The pointer will change shape and now be a black arrow.

	A ↓	B	C
1	Add these Numbers		
2	3		
3	6		
4	9		
5			

➔ Move your mouse over the line that separates Column A and Column B
➔ Your mouse pointer will change shape again, this time to a cross with arrows.

	A ↔	B	C
1	Add these Numbers		
2	3		
3	6		
4	9		
5			

➔ When you see the new shape, hold down your left mouse button.
➔ Keep the left mouse button held down and drag your cross to the right.
➔ Once you have all the text in the A column, let go of the left mouse button.

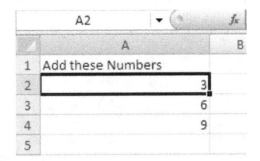

You can make the height of the Rows bigger or smaller by using the same technique.
The numbers, however, don't look very tidy. We'll now see how to center them, and the text as well.

1.8 HOW TO CENTRE TEXT AND NUMBERS

You saw that by clicking inside of a cell it makes it active, so that you can make changes. We want to Centre all our numbers and the text. Here's the spreadsheet we have:

So, we need cells A1, A2, A3 and A4 to be active. In Excel, you can do this by highlighting the cells.

- Place your mouse over cell A1.

- Your pointer should now be in the shape of a white cross.

- When your pointer changes to the white cross, hold your left mouse button down and drag to cell A4.

- Let go of the left mouse button when cells A1, A2, A3 and A4 are highlighted.

- The image below shows what you are aiming for.

	A	B	C	D
1	Add these Numbers			
2	3			
3	6			
4	9			
5				

A1 | fx | Add these Numbers

The cells highlighted in the image above have a different color to the normal white color of a cell. When you highlight cells, you can do things to all the cells as a group.

To Centre the text and numbers in our highlighted cells, try this:
From the Excel Ribbon at the top of the screen, locate the Alignment panel. Here's the Alignment panel in Excel:
You can see the various alignment options laid out. These ones:

Align

Hold your mouse over each alignment icon and you'll see an explanation of what they do. Click each icon and see what they do to your highlighted cells.
You can also click the arrow in the bottom right of the Alignment panel to bring up the Format Cells box.

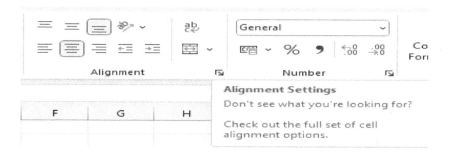

When you click the arrow, you'll see this dialogue box:

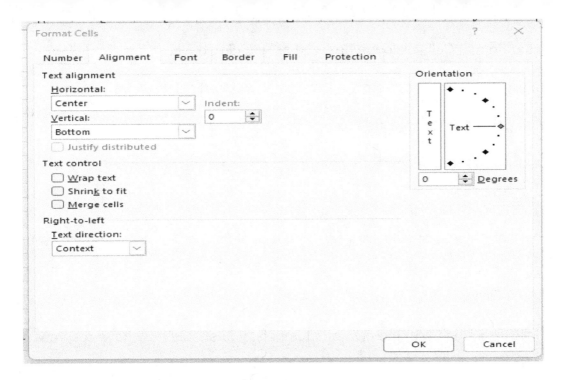

Notice the Text Alignment section at the top of the Alignment tab. It has two drop-down menus, one for Horizontal alignment and one for Vertical alignment.

- Click the arrow on the Horizontal drop-down menu, the one with Left (Indent) on it.
- You'll see the following:

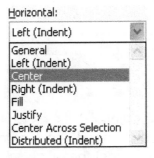

As you can see, you have plenty of options to choose from in Excel. But click on Center. Do the same for the Vertical drop-down menu. Then click OK at the bottom of the Format Cells dialogue box.

The text and numbers in cells A1, A2, A3 and A4 should now be centered, and your spreadsheet will look like the one below:

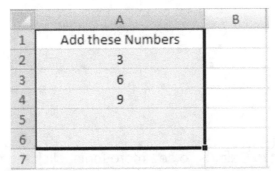

Before moving on to other types of formatting you can do in Excel, have a try of this:

- Highlight the cells A5 and A6 on your spreadsheet.

- Bring up the Format Cells dialogue box, just as you did above.

- Make the alignment changes from the Horizontal and Vertical drop-down menus.

- Click OK to get rid of the dialogue box.

- Now click inside of cell A5 on your spreadsheet and enter any number you like.

- Hit the Enter key.

The number you just entered should also be centered. So even if a cell is empty, you can still apply formatting to it.

1.9 FONT FORMATTING

If you've been following along with the previous tutorials, you should now have a spreadsheet that looks like this:

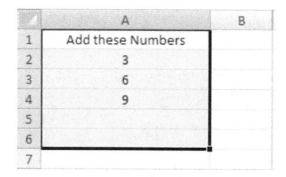

Choosing a Font in Excel

You can pick a different font for the data you enter cells, as well as choosing the size you want. The color of the font, and the cell background, can be changed, too. Themes have been introduced, so that you can format your spreadsheets more easily. You'll meet these later. First, we'll see how to change the font type.

- Highlight cell A1 on your spreadsheet by simply clicking into it.

- Locate the Font panel on the Excel Ribbon at the top of the page:

The font in the panel above is set to Calibri. To see more fonts, click the black down arrow:

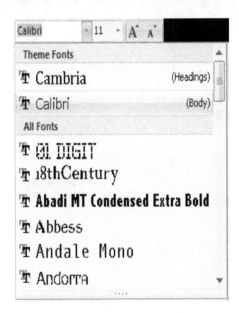

The good thing about this Excel is that when you move your mouse over one of the fonts on the list, the text in your selected cell (A1) will change automatically. This is just a preview, though. When you have decided on the font you want, click it with the left mouse button.

You can change the size of the font in the same way - just choose a new font size from the list of numbers in the drop-down box.

If you want to change the font via the Format Cells dialogue box, as you did in previous versions of Excel, you can click the small arrow in the bottom right of the Font panel:

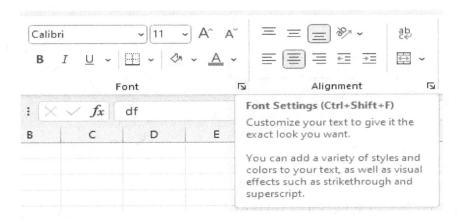

When you click the arrow, you'll see the Format Cells dialogue box. You can choose various options from this dialogue box: Font size, style, size, etc. The dialogue box looks like this:

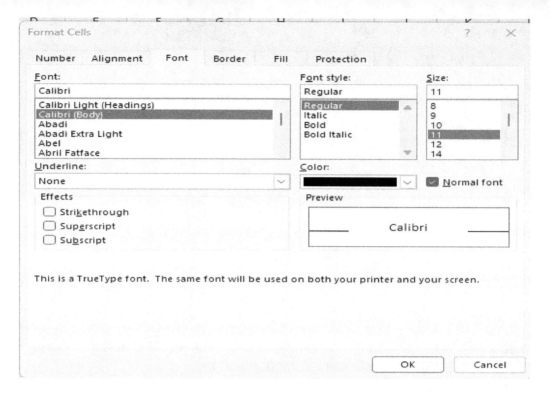

You can also set the font color from here and add text effects. Click OK when you have made your choices.

When you have changed the font and font size, your A1 cell might look something like this:

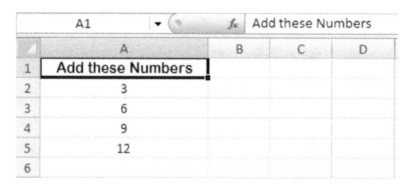

1.10 HOW TO CHANGE THE COLOUR OF A CELL

In the previous lesson, you saw how to change the font and font size in Excel. In this lesson, we'll look at how to change the color of a cell.

Change the Background Color of a Cell

- To change the background color of cells, you first must highlight the ones you want to alter. We'll start with the cells A2 to A5. So, highlight these cells on your spreadsheet.

- With the cells A2 to A5 highlighted, locate the Font panel on the Ribbon at the top of the Excel: (The image below is from Excel)

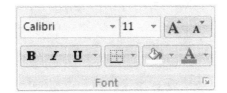

- Locate the Paint Bucket and click the arrow just to the right of it. You'll see some colors appear:

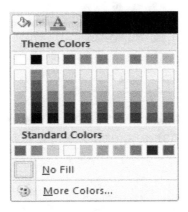

Move your mouse over any of the colors and the cells will change automatically. You can then see what the new color looks like. Click with the left mouse button to set the color you want. If you don't like any of the colors displayed, click on "More Colors".

Once you have the number cells formatted in a different color, click on the cell A1. Now do the same thing, only this time choose a contrasting color for the background of this cell. Your spreadsheet should then look something like the one below.

	A	B	C
1	**Add these Numbers**		
2	3		
3	6		
4	9		
5	12		
6			

Change The Text Color

To change the color of the text itself, click the down arrow just to the right of the letter A, which is just to the right of the Paint Bucket on the Font panel.

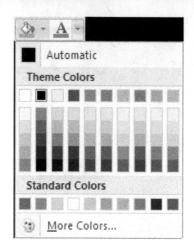

Select a color just like you did for the background color of the cell. Here's what your spreadsheet might look like with the background cell color changes, and the text color:

	A	B	C
1	Add these Numbers		
2	3		
3	6		
4	9		
5	12		
6			

1.11 HOW TO SAVE YOUR WORK IN EXCEL

Now that your spreadsheet is coming along nicely, you'll want to save your work. To save your spreadsheet, do the following.

- Click the File tab in the top left of the excel, This one:

When you click the File tab, you'll see the options list appear:

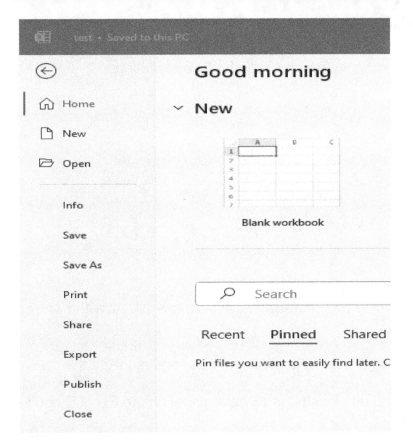

Click save as then choose Browse then the following dialogue box will appear:

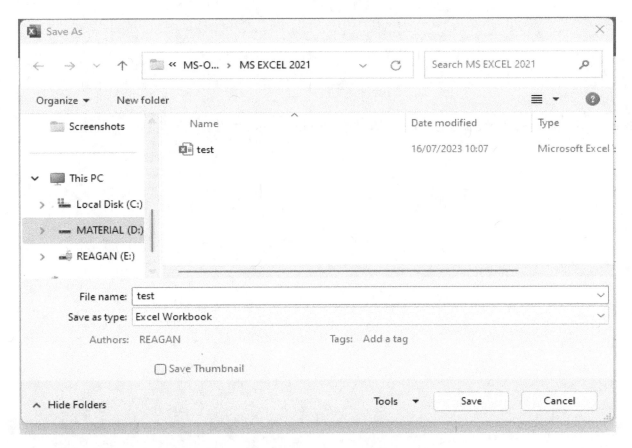

Type your name and then click save to finish save your document.

1.12 CURRENCY SYMBOLS IN EXCEL

Look at the following spreadsheet, which you'll shortly be creating:

	A	B	C	D
1		Shopping Bill		
2				
3	Item	Number	Price Each	
4	Mars Bars	4	£0.35	
5	Aeros	10	£0.32	
6	Twixes	4	£0.39	
7	Crisps	12	£0.35	
8	Pop	4	£0.59	
9				

The C column has a heading of "Price Each". The prices all have the currency symbol. To insert the currency symbol, do this:

- Enter some prices on a spreadsheet (any will do) and highlight the cells.

- With the cells highlighted, locate the Number panel on the Excel Ribbon bar (on the Home Tab):

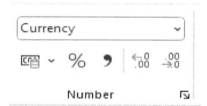

Click the drop-down list that says General. You'll then be presented with a list of options:

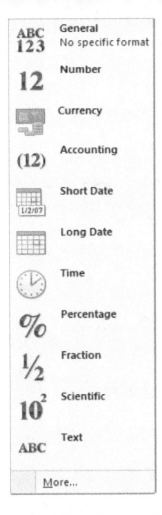

Click the Currency item to add a pound sign. But if you're not in the UK, you'll see the default currency for your country.

To see other currencies, click on More (or More Number Formats). The Format Cells dialogue box appears. In the Category list, click on Currency. Select a Currency sign from the Symbol list. The dialogue box will then look like this:

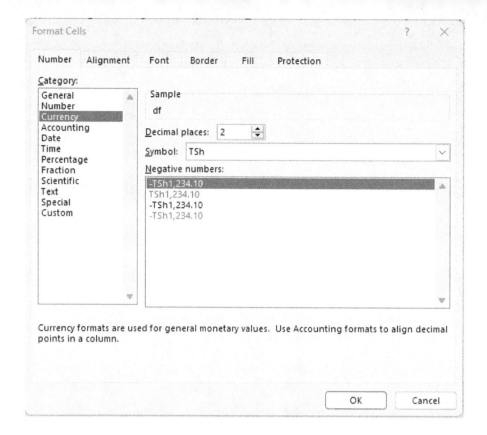

Click OK to set the pound sign as the currency.

1.13 HOW TO MERGE CELLS

Study the spreadsheet below:

	A	B	C	D
1	Shopping Bill			
2				
3	Item	Number	Price Each	
4	Mars Bars	4	£0.35	
5	Aeros	10	£0.32	
6	Twixes	4	£0.39	
7	Crisps	12	£0.35	
8	Pop	4	£0.59	
9				

If you look at Row 1, you'll see that the "Shopping Bill" heading stretches across three cells. This is not three separate cells, with a color change for each individual cell. The A1, B1 and C1 cells were merged. To merge cells, do the following.

- Type the words Shopping Bill into cell A1 of a spreadsheet.

- Highlight the cells A1, B1 and C1

- On the Alignment panel of the Excel Ribbon, locate the "Merge and Center" item:

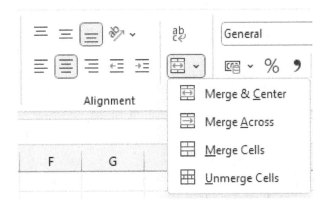

- Click on "Merge and Center". Your three cells will then become one - A1, to be exact!

PART TWO:

A MORE COMPLEX SPREADSHEET

2.1 INTRODUCTION

Now that you've gotten a feel for how Excel works, we'll build a more complex spreadsheet. The skills you'll learn in this section are:

- How to use AutoFill

- How to insert a row or a column

- How to add up numbers in a column

- And how to enter simple formulas for your calculations

The spreadsheet you'll construct looks like this when it's finished:

	A	B	C	D	E	F	G	H
1	My Chocolate Addiction							
2								
3		Monday	Tuesday	Wednesday	Thursday	Friday	Saturday	Sunday
4	Mars Bars	1	2	1	3	3	2	5
5	Twix	7	5	3	2	4	2	4
6	Bounty	8	3	2	3	4	1	4
7	Other	1	2	2	2	2	1	1
8								
9	Day Totals	17	12	8	10	13	6	14
10								

Not much has been done in the way of formatting here, as we'll concentrate on how to add up in Excel. To make a start, follow along with the instructions below.

- Click inside of cell A1 on a new spreadsheet.

- Type the text "My Chocolate Addiction", then press the Enter key on your keyboard.

- Highlight the cells A1, B1 and C1, and Merge the cells, just like you did for Review One

- Your spreadsheet will look like this in Excel 2007:

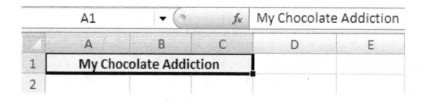

Now that you have a heading for your spreadsheet, we'll fill in the days of the week using something called AutoFill. This allows you to quickly fill in things like days of the week, months, and consecutive numbers.

2.2 HOW TO USE AUTOFILL

Your spreadsheet from the previous section should look like this one:

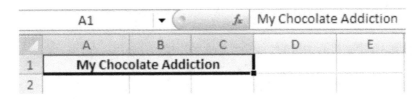

You have a title in cell A1, but nothing else. You'll now see how to use the AutoFill feature of Excel to quickly enter the days of the week.

Excel AutoFill

Click inside cell B3 of your spreadsheet, and type Monday, as in the image below:

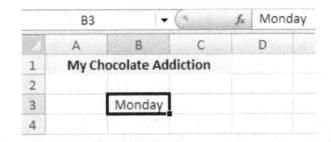

The days of the week are going to be entered on Row 3 of our spreadsheet, from cell B3 to cell H3. Fortunately, you don't have to type them all out. You can use something called AutoFill to complete a known sequence like days of the week. In other words, Excel will do it all for us.

- Position your mouse pointer to the bottom right of the B3 cell.
- The mouse pointer will change to a black cross, as in the images below. The image on the left shows the normal white cross; the image on the right, the black cross, tells you AutoFill is available:

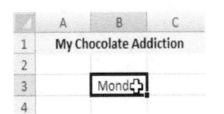 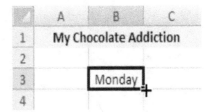

- When you can see the AutoFill cursor, hold down your left mouse button and drag to the right.

- Drag your mouse all the way to cell H3, as in the following image:

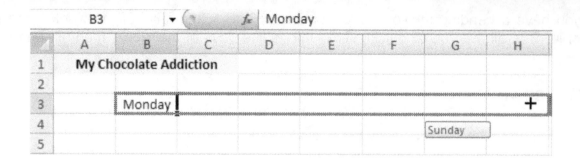

- When your cursor is in the H3 cell, let go of the left mouse button.

Excel will now complete the days of the week.

	A	B	C	D	E	F	G	H
1	My Chocolate Addiction							
2								
3		Monday	Tuesday	Wednesday	Thursday	Friday	Saturday	Sunday
4								

And that's all there is too it! AutoFill can be a handy tool to use, when you want to complete a known sequence like days of the week, months, and even formulas. We'll use AutoFill on a column of numbers, shortly. But let's crack on with our spreadsheet.
Now that we've got a heading for the spreadsheet, as well as the days of the week, we can enter a few chocolate bars.

- Click inside cell A4 and enter the name of a chocolate bar. You can enter anything you like, but we've gone for Mars Bars. In cell A5 we chose Twix, and in cell A6 Bounty. In cell A7 we typed Other

- In cell A9 of your spreadsheet enter the words Day Totals. Leave cell A8 blank. Your spreadsheet should then look something like ours below:

	A	B	C	D	E	F	G	H
1	My Chocolate Addiction							
2								
3		Monday	Tuesday	Wednesday	Thursday	Friday	Saturday	Sunday
4	Mars Bars							
5	Twix							
6	Bounty							
7	Other							
8								
9	Day Totals							

Time to enter some numbers.

- Click inside cell B4 and enter the number 1. Press the enter key on your keyboard, and the active cell will jump down to cell B5.

- In cell B5 type the number 7. Press the Enter key again to jump down to cell B6.

- In cell B6 type 8

- In cell B7 type 1

- Your spreadsheet will then look like this one:

	A	B	C	D	E	F	G	H
1	My Chocolate Addiction							
2								
3		Monday	Tuesday	Wednesday	Thursday	Friday	Saturday	Sunday
4	Mars Bars	1						
5	Twix	7						
6	Bounty	8						
7	Other	1						
8								
9	Day Totals							

To complete the numbers for the rest of the week, enter the following under each heading:
Tuesday: 2, 5, 3, 2
Wednesday: 1, 3, 2, 2
Thursday: 3, 2, 3, 2
Friday: 3, 4, 4, 2
Saturday: 2, 2, 1, 1
Sunday: 5, 4, 4, 1

When you're done, your spreadsheet will look like this:

	A	B	C	D	E	F	G	H
1	My Chocolate Addiction							
2								
3		Monday	Tuesday	Wednesday	Thursday	Friday	Saturday	Sunday
4	Mars Bars	1	2	1	3	3	2	5
5	Twix	7	5	3	2	4	2	4
6	Bounty	8	3	2	3	4	1	4
7	Other	1	2	2	2	2	1	1
8								
9	Day Totals							

2.3 ENTERING SIMPLE ADDITION FORMULA

The first thing we'll do to our spreadsheet from the previous section is to add up all those numbers, the ones going down under the days of the week headings. The total for each day of the week will be placed on Row 9. So, Monday's total will go in cell B9, Tuesday's total will go in cell C9, and so on.
Here's our spreadsheet again:

	A	B	C	D	E	F	G	H
1	My Chocolate Addiction							
2								
3		Monday	Tuesday	Wednesday	Thursday	Friday	Saturday	Sunday
4	Mars Bars	1	2	1	3	3	2	5
5	Twix	7	5	3	2	4	2	4
6	Bounty	8	3	2	3	4	1	4
7	Other	1	2	2	2	2	1	1
8								
9	Day Totals							

Our first total will go in cell B9.

Adding up in Excel

Excel needs to know which cells you want to add up. Look at the numbers for the Monday column. We have a 1 in cell B4, a 7 in cell B5, an 8 in cell B6, and a 1 in cell B7. So, we want the answer to this:
B4 + B5 + B6 + B7
To let Excel, know that this is what we want, try this:

- Click inside cell B9, which is where we want the answer to appear.

- Once you've clicked on cell B9, click into the formula bar at the top.

Type this:
B4 + B5 + B6 + B7
When you have entered the formula in the formula bar, press the enter key on your keyboard. Your spreadsheet should look like ours below:

B9	▼	f_x	B4 + B5 + B6 + B7

	A	B	C	D
1		My Chocolate Addiction		
2				
3		Monday	Tuesday	Wednesday
4	Mars Bars	1	2	1
5	Twix	7	5	3
6	Bounty	8	3	2
7	Other	1	2	2
8				
9	Day Totals	B4 + B5 + B6 + B7		
10				

Something has gone wrong! This is not quite what we were expecting. We wanted Excel to add up the numbers for us, but it hasn't done anything except enter the cells we typed.
What went wrong was that we didn't "tell" excel to add up. Excel needs you to type an equals (=) sign first, and then those cell references. If you don't include the equals sign, Excel thinks it's just plain text, and so doesn't do any calculating.
So, enter this inside of your formula bar instead:

= B4 + B5 + B6 + B7

In other words, put an equal's sign (=) before B4. Press your enter key and you should have the correct answer in cell B9.

Now click back inside the formula bar and delete the equal's sign. Press the enter key again. You should then just have the same text as in the image above. We're doing this to show you an easier way to add up - with the SUM function.

When your spreadsheet looks like ours in the image at the top of the page, you can move on to the next part.

2.4 THE SUM FUNCTION

You saw a simple way to add up in the previous section. Enter an equal's sign, followed by the cells you want Excel to add up:

= B4 + B5 + B6 + B7

But this is not a good way to add up in Excel: it could get very tedious indeed if you had to type out say 50 cell references by hand. The easy way is to get Excel to do the work for you. That's where SUM comes in.

The Excel SUM function

The SUM function is used to add things up and saves you the bother of typing out lots of cell names and numbers. It looks like this:

=SUM ()

In between the round brackets, you type what you want Excel to add up. Look at our spreadsheet again.

	A	B	C	D	E	F	G	H
1	My Chocolate Addiction							
2								
3		Monday	Tuesday	Wednesday	Thursday	Friday	Saturday	Sunday
4	Mars Bars	1	2	1	3	3	2	5
5	Twix	7	5	3	2	4	2	4
6	Bounty	8	3	2	3	4	1	4
7	Other	1	2	2	2	2	1	1
8								
9	Day Totals							

We want to add up the numbers under the Monday heading and place the answer in cell B9.

So, with cell B9 selected again, click into your formula bar. If you're following along from the previous lesson, you should have this in cell B9:

	B9		f_x	B4 + B5 + B6 + B7

	A	B	C	D
1		**My Chocolate Addiction**		
2				
3		Monday	Tuesday	Wednesday
4	Mars Bars	1	2	1
5	Twix	7	5	3
6	Bounty	8	3	2
7	Other	1	2	2
8				
9	Day Totals	B4 + B5 + B6 + B7		
10				

If you have an equal's sign before B4, delete it and press the enter key. Now position your cursor at the start of the line, before the "B" of B4.

Type an equal's sign first, then the letter SU of SUM.

As soon as you start typing, Excel will present you with a drop-down list of available functions. Click once with the left mouse button on SUM to highlight it:

=SuB4 + B5 + B6 + B7			
f_x SUBSTITUTE	E	F	G
f_x SUBTOTAL			
f_x SUM	Adds all the numbers in a range of cells		
f_x SUMIF			
f_x SUMIFS	Thursday	Friday	Saturday	S
f_x SUMPRODUCT	3	3	2
f_x SUMSQ	2	4	2
f_x SUMX2MY2	3	4	1
f_x SUMX2PY2	2	2	1
f_x SUMXMY2			

Now double click on SUM. Excel will add the "M" for you, and the left bracket. It will also highlight the cells in your formula:

	SUM		X ✓ f_x	=SUM(B4 + B5 + B6 + B7
				SUM(number1, [number2], ...)

	A	B	C		
1		**My Chocolate Addiction**			
2					
3		Monday	Tuesday	Wednesday	Thursday
4	Mars Bars	1	2	1	3
5	Twix	7	5	3	2
6	Bounty	8	3	2	3
7	Other	1	2	2	2
8					
9	Day Totals	=SUM(B4 + B5 +			
10					

Now press the Enter key on your keyboard. Excel will add the right bracket, and work out the SUM for you:

	B9			f_x	=SUM(B4 + B5 + B6 + B7)

	A	B	C	D	E
1		**My Chocolate Addiction**			
2					
3		Monday	Tuesday	Wednesday	Thursday
4	Mars Bars	1	2	1	3
5	Twix	7	5	3	2
6	Bounty	8	3	2	3
7	Other	1	2	2	2
8					
9	Day Totals	17			
10					

Now click back on cell B9 and look at the Name box (just above the A column, in our image). It has B9 in it. The formula bar to the right shows you which formula you have in the active cell (B9).
An easier way to add up number with the SUM function is to use a colon (:) The colon is a shorthand way of adding up consecutive cells. Instead of typing out all those cell references like this:

=SUM (B4 + B5 + B6 + B7)

You can just type out the first cell reference, then a colon, then the last cell reference. Like this:

=Sum (B4: B7)

Excel will then add up the numbers in cells B4 to B7. It knows what the colon means!

- Click into cell B9 if it's not already active.

- Now click on the cell with your right mouse button

- You'll see a menu appear:

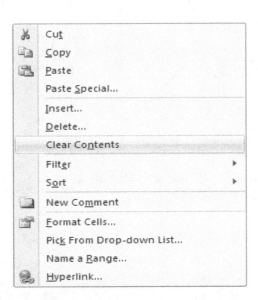

- From the menu, select Clear Contents by clicking the item with your left mouse button.

- This will clear the formula from the formula bar.

- Now click back inside of the formula bar and type the following:

= Sum (B4:B7)
Your spreadsheet should look like ours:

SUM	▾	× ✓ ƒx	=SUM(B4:B7)

	A	B	C	D
1		My Chocolate Addiction		
2				
3		Monday	Tuesday	Wednesday
4	Mars Bars	1	2	1
5	Twix	7	5	3
6	Bounty	8	3	2
7	Other	1	2	2
8				
9	Day Totals	=SUM(B4:B7)		
10				

When you have the formula typed out, hit the Enter key on your keyboard. Excel will add up the numbers for you and place the correct answer in cell B9.
If everything went well, you should have an answer of 17 in cell B9. Fortunately, we can use AutoFill for the rest of the answers.

- Place your mouse pointer to the bottom right of cell B9.

- The pointer will turn into a thin black cross:

	A	B	C	D	E	F	G	H
1		My Chocolate Addiction						
2								
3		Monday	Tuesday	Wednesday	Thursday	Friday	Saturday	Sunday
4	Mars Bars	1	2	1	3	3	2	5
5	Twix	7	5	3	2	4	2	4
6	Bounty	8	3	2	3	4	1	4
7	Other	1	2	2	2	2	1	1
8								
9	Day Totals	17						
10								

- Hold down your left mouse button.

- Keep it held down, and drag your mouse to cell H9:

	A	B	C	D	E	F	G	H
1	**My Chocolate Addiction**							
2								
3		Monday	Tuesday	Wednesday	Thursday	Friday	Saturday	Sunday
4	Mars Bars	1	2	1	3	3	2	5
5	Twix	7	5	3	2	4	2	4
6	Bounty	8	3	2	3	4	1	4
7	Other	1	2	2	2	2	1	1
8								
9	Day Totals	17						
10								

With your mouse pointer over cell H9, let go of the left button. Excel will AutoFill the rest of the formulas. It uses the same formula from cell B9 to get the answers, and just alters all the cell references. Without AutoFill, you'd have to type it all out yourself!

The answers on Row 9 of your spreadsheet should be the same as ours in the image below:

H9			f_x	=SUM(H4:H7)			

	A	B	C	D	E	F	G	H
1	**My Chocolate Addiction**							
2								
3		Monday	Tuesday	Wednesday	Thursday	Friday	Saturday	Sunday
4	Mars Bars	1	2	1	3	3	2	5
5	Twix	7	5	3	2	4	2	4
6	Bounty	8	3	2	3	4	1	4
7	Other	1	2	2	2	2	1	1
8								
9	Day Totals	17	12	8	10	13	6	14
10								

Notice the formula bar in the image. It shows the formula in cell H9. This is:
=Sum (H4:H7)

The formula we started with was:
=Sum (B4:B7)

Excel has changed the letters for us, but not the numbers. In other words, it's adding up the columns. If you think of the colon as the word TO, it should make sense:
Add up the cells B4 TO B7
Add up the cells H4 TO H7
In the next section, you'll get some more practice with this spreadsheet, and with the SUM Function. So don't forget to save the work you've done so far!

2.5 THE MORE SUM FUNCTION

Using the same spreadsheet, you've been working on in the previous section, you'll now get some more practice with the SUM function in Excel, to add up values in cells. Our spreadsheet now looks like this, though:

	H9		f_x	=SUM(H4:H7)				

	A	B	C	D	E	F	G	H
1	My Chocolate Addiction							
2								
3		Monday	Tuesday	Wednesday	Thursday	Friday	Saturday	Sunday
4	Mars Bars	1	2	1	3	3	2	5
5	Twix	7	5	3	2	4	2	4
6	Bounty	8	3	2	3	4	1	4
7	Other	1	2	2	2	2	1	1
8								
9	Day Totals	17	12	8	10	13	6	14
10								

You've just used the easy way to add up values in consecutive cells for a column. Just do this:
= SUM (B4:B7)

Using that formula gave us the answer to how many chocolate bars we ate from Monday to Sunday. You can use this same colon (:) shorthand to add up numbers in a Row.

- Click inside cell J3 of your Chocolate Addiction spreadsheet.

- Type the text Individual Totals (you may have to widen the column a bit, as you did for a previous section)

- Your spreadsheet will then look like this:

	J3		f_x	Individual Totals						

	A	B	C	D	E	F	G	H	I	J
1	My Chocolate Addiction									
2										
3		Monday	Tuesday	Wednesday	Thursday	Friday	Saturday	Sunday		Individual Totals
4	Mars Bars	1	2	1	3	3	2	5		
5	Twix	7	5	3	2	4	2	4		
6	Bounty	8	3	2	3	4	1	4		
7	Other	1	2	2	2	2	1	1		
8										
9	Day Totals	17	12	8	10	13	6	14		
10										

We'll use a SUM formula to add up the values in each Row. This will tell us how many of a particular chocolate bar we ate in one week: how many Mars Bars, how many Twix, etc.
The first answer we'll try is how many Mars Bars we ate in one week. We'll place this answer in cell J4. The cells we're going to be adding up are these:
B4 + C4 + D4 + E4 + F4 + G4 + H4

Because we have consecutive cells, we can use the colon shorthand again.
- Click into cell J4 of your spreadsheet.

- Then click into the formula bar at the top.

- Enter the following formula:

= Sum (B4:H4)

Press the enter key on your keyboard, and you'll see the answer appear in J4. To complete the rest of the rows, we can use AutoFill again.

- Click back in cell J4 to make it the active cell.

- Move your mouse pointer to the bottom right of cell J4.

- You'll see the pointer change to a thin black cross:

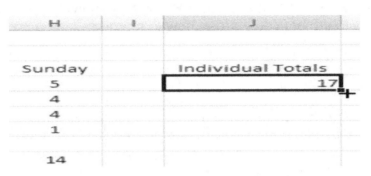

- Now hold down your left mouse button
- Keep the left button held down and drag down to cell J7.

H	I	J
Sunday		Individual Totals
5		17
4		
4		
1		
14		

When your mouse pointer gets to cell J7, let go of the left button. Excel will use AutoFill to get the answers for the other three cells. Hopefully, your spreadsheet now looks like ours:

J
Individual Totals
17
27
25
11

Select any of the cells J4, J5, J6 and J7. Then examine the formula in the formula bar. You should be able to understand what is being added up, and what all the formulas mean.

Now that we have totals for each individual chocolate bar, we can work out how many chocolate bars we ate for the whole week. We'll put the Grand Total in cell F11. First, we'll enter some text to explain what is being added up.

- Click inside cell A11 on your spreadsheet.

- Type the following text: Number of Chocolate bars consumed in a week.

- Hit the Enter key on your keyboard.

- You should see the text you just typed. But it will all be in individual cells. Highlight the cells A11 to E11 and merge them together (You learned how to merge cells in a previous section.)

- This is what your spreadsheet should now look like:

	A	B	C	D	E	F	G	H	I	J
1	My Chocolate Addiction									
2										
3		Monday	Tuesday	Wednesday	Thursday	Friday	Saturday	Sunday		Individual Totals
4	Mars Bars	1	2	1	3	3	2	5		17
5	Twix	7	5	3	2	4	2	4		27
6	Bounty	8	3	2	3	4	1	4		25
7	Other	1	2	2	2	2	1	1		11
8										
9	Day Totals	17	12	8	10	13	6	14		
10										
11	Number of Chocolate bars consumed in a week									
12										

There are two ways we can calculate the Grand Total. You can just add up the Individual totals in the J column, or ... Well, how else could you get the number of chocolate bars consumed in one week?

- Click into cell F11 on your spreadsheet!

- Enter your formula to calculate the number of chocolate bars consumed in one week.

- Hit the Enter key when you think you have the correct formula.

The correct answer is 80. If you got a different answer or are struggling in any way to come up with the correct formula, then it's a good idea to go over the previous section. But don't just type 80 into cell F11 and move on!

2.6 COPYING AND PASTING IN EXCEL

OK, 80 chocolate bars in one week is a lot of chocolate bars. But how much is this addiction costing every week? How much is it costing per year?
We can work this sum out quite easily. First, we'll need some text headings.

- Click inside cell A13 and enter the text "Cost of Addiction."

- Merge the text into one cell, just like you did in the last part.

- Format the text: bold, center, a colored font or background if you prefer

- When you have finished, press the Return key on your keyboard.

We'll now copy and paste some text.

- Click inside cell A4, then highlighted the cells down to A7 (the cells A4, A5, A6 and A7 should be highlighted)

- From the menu bar, click on Edit.

- From the menu that drops down, click copy.

- There should be some sort of animated line around your highlighted cells - the marching ants!

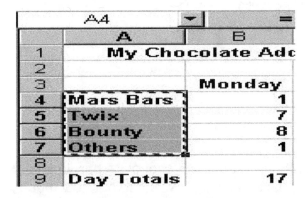

- When you see the marching ants, click inside cell A15 of your spreadsheet.

- Press the Return key on your keyboard.

- The text should have been copied to the new location, and your spreadsheet will look like the one below.

		Monday	Tuesday	Wednesday	Thursday
1	My Chocolate Addiction				
2					
3		Monday	Tuesday	Wednesday	Thursday
4	Mars Bars	1	2	1	3
5	Twix	7	5	3	2
6	Bounty	8	3	2	3
7	Others	1	2	2	2
8					
9	Day Totals	17	12	8	10
10					
11	Number of Chocolate bars consumed in a week:				
12					
13	Cost of Addiction				
14					
15	Mars Bars				
16	Twix				
17	Bounty				
18	Others				
19					

We'll enter some more headings, so that we can work out how much this addiction is costing.

- Click inside cell B14 and enter Price.

- Click inside cell C14 and enter Number.

- Click inside cell D14 and enter Cost.

The spreadsheet now looks like this:

	A	B	C	D	E
1	My Chocolate Addiction				
2					
3		Monday	Tuesday	Wednesday	Thursday
4	Mars Bars	1	2	1	3
5	Twix	7	5	3	2
6	Bounty	8	3	2	3
7	Others	1	2	2	2
8					
9	Day Totals	17	12	8	10
10					
11	Number of Chocolate bars consumed in a week:				
12					
13	Cost of Addiction				
14		Price	Number	Cost	
15	Mars Bars				
16	Twix				
17	Bounty				
18	Others				
19					

Under "Price" is where we'll put the price of each chocolate bar. Under "Number" we'll put the number of each bar eaten in a week. Under "Cost" is where we'll find out how much is being spent each week on the individual chocolate bars. In other words, how much is being spent on Mars Bars, how much on Twix, how much on Bounty Bars, and how much on others.
So, enter some prices. Our researchers have been out and about eating chocolate bars. They found that prices for each chocolate bar are these:

Mars Bars .35
Twix .29
Bounty .32
Others .40

So, enter those numbers in the price's column. Don't forget to put "dot price" and not just "price". So, it would be .35 for mars bars and not just 35.
When you have finished entering the prices, you can format them all as Currency. You learnt how these in the first section do. (Format > Cells, then click the Number tab strip form the dialogue box. Click Currency under Category, and format it to 2 decimal places.

2.7 PASTE SPECIAL

In the previous section, you created new areas of your spreadsheet that look like this:

13	Cost of Addiction			
14		Price	Number	Cost
15	Mars Bars	£0.35		
16	Twix	£0.29		
17	Bounty	£0.32		
18	Other	£0.40		
19				

We have prices in the B column. Under the Number heading, we're going to put how many of each chocolate bar we ate in one week: how many Mars Bars we ate will go in cell C15, how many Twix will go in cell C16, how many Bounty bars will go in cell C17, and how many other chocolate bars we ate will go in cell C18.
But we already have the weekly totals elsewhere in the spreadsheet, so we don't need to calculate them all over again. We can Copy and Paste the formula over to cells C15, C16, C17 and C18.

Paste Special in Excel

We have the weekly totals for each chocolate bar in the J column, under the Individual Totals heading.

- So, highlight your four totals in the J column of your spreadsheet.

- From the Clipboard panel, click Copy.

- You'll see the marching ants again:

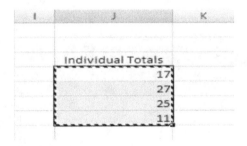

- Now, under the Numbers heading, click into cell C15.
- Press the enter key on your keyboard to paste the numbers across
- What you should notice is that something has gone wrong!

13	Cost of Addiction			
14		Price	Number	Cost
15	Mars Bars	⧫35	#REF!	
16	Twix	£0.29	#REF!	
17	Bounty	£0.32	#REF!	
18	Other	£0.40	#REF!	
19				

So, what happened? Why have all those strange #REF comments appeared in the cells?
If you hold your mouse over the exclamation mark in the yellow diamond, you'll see this:

Moving or deleting cells caused an invalid cell reference, or function is returning reference error.

That complex error message means that Excel tried to paste the formulas over. But the cell references it has been all for the J column.
To solve the problem, we can paste the values over and not the formula.

- Click the left curved arrow at the very top of Excel to Undo (or press CTRL + Z on your keyboard)

- Highlight the four cells in the J column again.

- From the Clipboard panel, click copy.

- Highlight the cells C15 to C18
- Using your right mouse button, click anywhere in the highlighted area. You'll see the following menu in Excel:

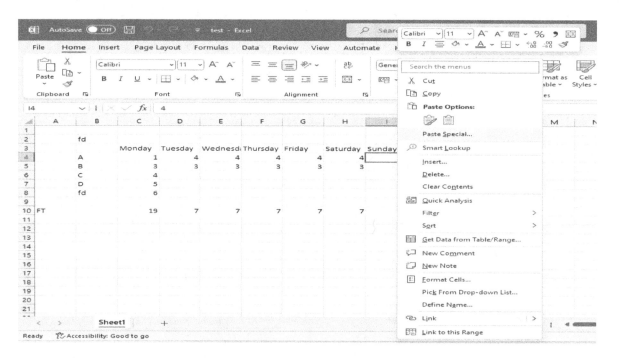

- From the menu, click Paste Special with your left mouse button.
- The Paste Special dialogue box will appear:

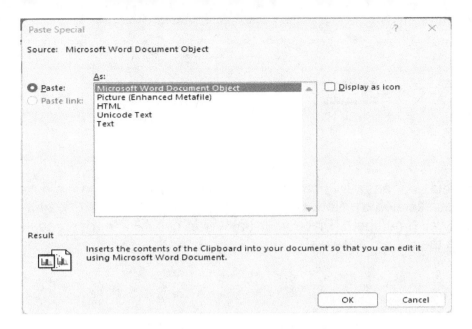

Now that we have a price for each chocolate bar, and how many we are eating each week, we can calculate how much our addiction is costing us. For that, we'll need to multiply.

HOW TO MULTIPLY IN EXCEL

In an earlier section, you saw how to multiply two numbers. You use the asterisk symbol between two cell references:
= A4 * B5

If you need to multiply more than two numbers, you don't have to do this:
= A4 * A5 * A6 * A7 * A8

You can use the colon (:) notation to shorten the formula. With addition, you used the word SUM, and placed your formula between round brackets:
= SUM (A4:A8)
With multiplication, you can use the word PRODUCT instead. Like this:
= PRODUCT (A4:A8)

The only thing that has changed here is the name of the inbuilt function: PRODUCT instead of SUM. But Excel will see the word Product and multiply whatever is between the round brackets.
You can use PRODUCT in the same way you did for SUM. For example, if you wanted to add up values in cells A4 to A8, and cells B4 and B5, you'd do it like this:

= PRODUCT (A4:A8, B4, B5)
To give you some practice, try these exercises.

Exercise

On a new worksheet, enter the number 1, 2, 3, 4 and 5. Put them into cells A1 to E1. Now use PRODUCT to multiply all five numbers. Place your answer in cell A3. If you get it right, your spreadsheet should look like ours:

	A	B	C	D	E
1	1	2	3	4	5
2					
3	120				
4					

Exercise

For this exercise, delete your answer in cell A3. (You can do this by clicking into cell A3, and then hitting the Delete key on your keyboard). Now type a 6 in cell A3, a 7 in cell C3, and an 8 in cell E3. Use PRODUCT to multiply all 8 numbers. Place your answer in cell A5. Your spreadsheet will look like ours below when you have the correct answer:

	A	B	C	D	E
1	1	2	3	4	5
2					
3	6		7		8
4					
5	40320				
6					

2.8 SUBTRACTION IN EXCEL

You saw that to subtract one number from another, you just use the minus sign:
= A1 - A2
The image below shows the value in cell A2 being deducted from the value in cell A1. The formula has been entered in cell A3.

A3			f_x	= A1 - B1	
	A	B	C	D	E
1	25	14			
2					
3	11				
4					

If you want to subtract more than two cells you can do it like this:
= A1 - B1 - C1

In a later section, you'll see why that formula may not give you the answer you were expecting. But subtraction in Excel is straightforward and shouldn't cause you too many problems.

2.9 DIVISION IN EXCEL

Dividing one value from another involves using the forward slash symbol (/). An example of its use is this:
= A1 / C1

Here, we're just telling Excel to divide the cell value on the left of the slash symbol by the cell value on the right. Division is straightforward, too.

You can combine all the basic arithmetic operators to produce more complex formulas. We'll see how to do that now.

2.10 COMBINING ARITHMETIC OPERATORS

The basic operators you've just met can be combined to make more complex calculations. For example, you can add to cells together, and multiply by a third one. Like this:
= A1 + A2 * A3
Or this:
= A1 + A2 - A3

And even this:
=SUM (A1:A9) * B1

In the above formula, we're asking Excel to add up the numbers in the cells A1 to A9, and then multiply the answer by B1. You'll get some practice with combining the operators shortly. But there's something you need to be aware of called Operator Precedence.

Operator Precedence

Some of the operators you have just met are calculated before others. This is known as Operator Precedence. As an example, try this:

- Open a new Excel spreadsheet.

- In cell A1 enter 25

- In cell A2 enter 50

- In cell A3 enter 2

Now click in cell A5 and enter the following formula:
= (A1 + A2) * A3

Hit the enter key on your keyboard, and you'll see an answer of 150.
The thing to pay attention to here is the brackets. When you place brackets around cell references, you section these cells off. Excel will then work out the answer to your formula inside of the brackets, A1 + A2 in our formula. Once it has the answer to whatever is inside of your round brackets, it will move on and calculate the rest of your formula. For us, this was multiplied by 3. So, Excel is doing this:

- Add up the A1 and A2 in between the round brackets.

- Multiply that answer by A3.

Now try this:

- Click inside A5 where your formula is.

- Now click into the formula bar at the top

- Delete the two round brackets.

- Hit the enter key on your keyboard.

What answer did you get? The images below show the answers with brackets and without:

With Brackets

A5	▼	f_x	= (A1 + A2) * A3

	A	B	C	D	E
1	25				
2	50				
3	2				
4					
5	150				
6					

Without Brackets

A5	▼	f_x	= A1 + A2 * A3

	A	B	C	D	E
1	25				
2	50				
3	2				
4					
5	125				
6					

So why did Excel give you two different answers? The reason it did so is because of operator precedence. Excel sees multiplication as more important than adding up, so it does that first. Without the brackets, our formula is this:
A1 + A2 * A3

You and I may work out the answer to that formula from left to right. So, we'll add A1 + A2, and THEN multiply by A3. But because Excel sees multiplication as more important, it will do the calculation this way:

- Multiply A2 by A3 first

- THEN add the A1

We have 50 in cell A2, and in cell A3 we have the number 2. When you multiply 50 by 2 you get 100. Add the 25 in cell A1 and the answer is 125.
When we used the brackets, we forced Excel to do the addition first:
(A1 + A2) * A3
Add the 25 in cell A1 to the 50 in cell A2 and your get 75. Now multiply by the 2 in cell A3 and you 150.
One answer is not more correct than the other. But because of operator precedence it meant that the multiplication got done first, then the addition. We had to used round brackets to tell Excel what we wanted doing first. Here's another example of operator precedence.

Substitute the asterisk symbol from your formula above with the division symbol. So instead of this:
= (A1 + A2) * A3

the formula will be this:
= (A1 + A2) / A3
When you hit the enter key on your keyboard, you should get an answer of 37.5.
Now click into cell A5, and then click into the formula bar. Delete the two round brackets and hit the enter key again. What answer did you get this time? Here's the two images:

With the brackets

A5			f_x = (A1 + A2) / A3		
	A	B	C	D	E
1	25				
2	50				
3	2				
4					
5	37.5				
6					

Without the brackets

A5			f_x = A1 + A2 / A3		
	A	B	C	D	E
1	25				
2	50				
3	2				
4					
5	50				
6					

Just like multiplication, division is seen as more important than addition. So, this will get done first. Without the brackets, Excel will first divide A2 by A3. When it has the answer, it will then add the A1. We used the round brackets to force Excel to calculate things differently. Hence the two different answers. One final example.
Change your formula in cell A5 to this:
= (A1 * A2) / A3

Hit the enter key, and you should get an answer of 625.
Again, remove the brackets, and hit the enter key. You'll still have an answer of 625. That's because Excel treats multiplication the same as division: they have equal importance. When this happens, Excel will work out the answer from left to right.
Addition and subtraction are also seen as equal. Try this formula in cell A5:
= A1 + A2 - A3

Now put some round brackets in. Try this first:
= (A1 + A2) - A3
And then see what happens when you try this:
= A1 + (A2 - A3)

Was there any difference? There shouldn't have been. You should have the same answer.
So, keep Operator Precedence in mind - all sums are not treated equally!
To give you some practice with combination formulas, have a go at constructing the more complex Budget spreadsheet in the link below.

2.11 A BUDGET SPREADSHEET

In the small town of Ever crease, the Council managed to collect half a million pounds from its citizens. Unfortunately, the Council spent all of this, and another 69 thousand besides. Naturally, the good people of Ever crease objected to being asked for another 69 thousand pounds. So, they got rid of the council and appointed a new one. Have a look at last year's budget and see if you can do better. Here's the budget where the previous council overspent by 69 thousand pounds:

	A	B	C	D	E	F	G
1	Budget	500,000					
2							
3	Salaries			Number		Total	
4	Police Officers	£16,000		3		48000	
5	Ambulance drivers	£12,000		2		24000	
6	Firemen/women	£15,000		2		30000	
7	School teachers	£16,000		5		80000	
8	Refuse collectors	£14,000		3		42000	
9	Your salary	£11,000		1		11000	
10							
11	Total Cost Salaries	£235,000					
12	Money Left	£265,000					
13							
14	Equipment and Costs			Number		Total	
15	Police Cars	5000		4		20000	
16	Ambulances	10000		2		20000	
17	Fire engines	12000		2		24000	
18	Bin Lorry	12000		2		24000	
19	School Books	200		55		11000	
20							
21	Total Cost Equipment	£99,000					
22	Money Left	£166,000					
23							
24	Extras			Number		Total	
25	Village care	20000		1		20000	
26	Fairs and Fetes	50000		1		50000	
27	Concerts(indoors)	30000		2		60000	
28	Concerts(outdoors)	50000		2		100000	
29	Ducks	200		10		2000	
30	Swans	500		6		3000	
31							
32	Total Cost Extras	235000					
33	Final Budget	-£ 69,000.00					
34	Total Spending	£ 569,000.00					
35	Monthly Spending	£ 47,416.67					
36	Budget Minus Extras	£ 334,000.00					
37							

The final budget figure is in cell B33. It says minus £69 000. Your job is to construct the same budget as above but making sure that you do not have a minus figure in cell B33. Otherwise, the people will fire you as well!
The first thing to do is to create the budget exactly as you see it above. When you have the same figures as in the image, you can then start to amend things. For example, do you really need all those ducks and

swans? What happens to your budget if you reduce the number of teachers from 5 to 4? Or the number of police cars from 4 to 2?

As soon as you make your reductions, you should see the figure in cell B33 change. At least it will if you have entered the correct formulas! Here's a little help on the formulas you need.

Budget Help

The first thing to do is to enter a figure of 500 000 in cell B1. This is the budget - how much is available to spend. You'll be referring to this figure in later cells. Then start on the budget sections.

The first section is Salaries. In the cells A4 to A9, enter the same labels as our image (Police Officers, Ambulance Drivers, etc.). Enter the salaries in cells B4 to B9. In cells D4 to D9, enter how many of each are on the payroll. In cells F4 to F9, enter a formula to work out the cost of each profession. So, 3 Police Officers multiplied by £16 000 is ...?

In cells B11, calculate the total cost of the salaries. In cell B12, calculate how much you have left to spend once the salaries have been deducted.

Do the same for the Equipment and Costs section. When you get to cell B22, you need to add the Salaries to the Equipment and Costs. Then you need to deduct your answer from the budget in cell B1. A combination formula will get you this.

The main calculations are in cells B32 to B36. For cell B32, calculate the total cost of the extras. For cell B33, this is just the Money Left. You then need to work out your Total Spending, how much you are spending each month. And the budget minus all those extras.

There is a lot of work to do with this spreadsheet. But completing it will bring your Excel skills on a lot!

2.12 FINISHING THE SPREADSHEET

To finish off the Excel spreadsheet you have been working on in this section, we'll add figures for the weekly cost and yearly costs of the chocolate addiction. We'll use AutoFill and SUM.

The bottom of our spreadsheet looks like this:

		Price	Number	Cost		80
11	Number of Chocolate bars consumed in a week:					80
12						
13	Cost of Addiction					
14		Price	Number	Cost		
15	Mars Bars	0.35	17	£5.95		
16	Twix	0.29	27	£7.83		
17	Bounty	0.32	25	£8.00		
18	Other	0.40	11	£4.40		
19						

We now have how much each individual chocolate bar is costing us each week. The next things to do are to add them all up to arrive at a weekly figure for all chocolate bars.

To calculate the weekly cost of the chocolate addiction, you can use the Excel SUM function. But there's an even easier way - use Auto Fill and SUM. Try this.

- Click inside cell F20.

- Click inside the Formula bar at the top and enter = SU

- When you see the drop-down list of functions, double click SUM.

- Now click inside D15 of your spreadsheet

- Excel will enter the Cell for you in the formula bar:

SUM	▾	× ✓ *fx*	=SUM(D15			

	A	B	C	SUM(number1, [number2], ...) F	G	H
13	Cost of Addiction					
14		Price	Number	Cost		
15	Mars Bars	0.35	17	£5.95		
16	Twix	0.29	27	£7.83		
17	Bounty	0.32	25	£8.00		
18	Other	0.40	11	£4.40		
19						
20	Weekly Cost of Chocolate Addiction:			JM(D15		
21						

- Notice the marching ants around Cell D15, and that there is a blue border with blue squares.

- Hold your mouse over the bottom right blue square until your cursor changes to a double-headed arrow.

Number	Cost
17	£5.95
27	£7.83

- Now hold your left mouse button down and drag down to cell D18.

- Let go and Excel will enter the rest of the formula for you:

SUM	▾	× ✓ *fx*	=SUM(D15:D18		

	A	B	C	SUM(number1, [number2], ...) F	G
13	Cost of Addiction				
14		Price	Number	Cost	
15	Mars Bars	0.35	17	£5.95	
16	Twix	0.29	27	£7.83	
17	Bounty	0.32	25	£8.00	
18	Other	0.40	11	£4.40	
19					
20	Weekly Cost of Chocolate Addiction:			)15:D18	
21					

Press the enter key on your keyboard to finish off the rest of the formula:

	F20		▼	f_x	=SUM(D15:D18)					
	A	B	C	D	E	F	G	H	I	J
1	My Chocolate Addiction									
2										
3		Monday	Tuesday	Wednesday	Thursday	Friday	Saturday	Sunday		Individual Totals
4	Mars Bars	1	2	1	3	3	2	5		17
5	Twix	7	5	3	2	4	2	4		27
6	Bounty	8	3	2	3	4	1	4		25
7	Other	1	2	2	2	2	1	1		11
8										
9	Day Totals	17	12	8	10	13	6	14		
10										
11		Number of Chocolate bars consumed in a week:				80				
12										
13	Cost of Addiction									
14		Price	Number	Cost						
15	Mars Bars	0.35	17	£5.95						
16	Twix	0.29	27	£7.83						
17	Bounty	0.32	25	£8.00						
18	Other	0.40	11	£4.40						
19										
20	Weekly Cost of Chocolate Addiction:					£26.18				
21										

If you did that correctly, you should have a figure of 26.18 in cell F20. That's how much our chocolate bar addiction is costing each week.

To work out how much the addiction is costing every year, we can multiply the weekly cost of the addiction by 52 (the number of weeks in a year). First, enter some suitable text in cell A21, something like "Annual Cost of Chocolate addiction". The answer can then go in cell F21, under the weekly cost.

- Click into cell F21 on your spreadsheet.

- Then click into the formula bar at the top.

- Enter the following.

= F20 * 52

Hit the enter key on your keyboard, and the correct answer should appear.
Cell F20 is where the weekly total is. Excel already knows what formula is inside of this cell, so only the cell reference is needed. After the multiply symbol, we then only need to enter the number of weeks in a year.
The answer you should have in cell F21 is 1, 361.36. Your spreadsheet should look like ours below:

13	Cost of Addiction				
14		Price	Number	Cost	
15	Mars Bars	0.35	17	£5.95	
16	Twix	0.29	27	£7.83	
17	Bounty	0.32	25	£8.00	
18	Other	0.40	11	£4.40	
19					
20	Weekly Cost of Chocolate Addiction:				£26.18
21	Annual Cost of Chocolate Addiction:				£1,361.36
22					
23					

The formula we just used mixes a cell reference with a number. Excel doesn't mind you doing it this way, just if there's something to multiply. So, you can do things this way:
= 26.18 * 52
Or this way:
= F20 * 52
If you have the number 52 typed into, say cell H20, you could just do this:
= F20 * H20
Whichever way you choose, though, just remember to use the asterisk to multiply things.

2.13 ADD A COMMENT TO A CELL

A comment can be added to any cell on your spreadsheet. When you hover your mouse pointer over a cell that contains a comment, you'll see the comment appear in a sort of Sticky-Note. To see how they work, study the spreadsheet below:

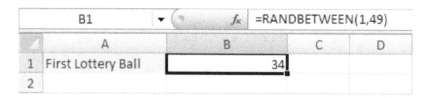

The formula in cell B1 above gives you a random number from 1 to 49. A new number can be had by clicking the "Calculate Now" button on the Formula menu.
To let users, know what to do, we'll add a comment to cell B1.
First, create the spreadsheet above. In cell B2, enter the following formula:
=RANDBETWEEN (1, 49)
The formula will generate a Random number between 1 and 49. Once you have the above spreadsheet up and running, click inside B1 and try it out:

- From the menu bars on the Ribbon at the top of Excel, click on Formula.

- Locate the Calculation panel, and then click on Calculate Now:

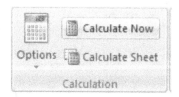

Excel will refresh the calculation and enter a new random number for you. To let people, know about this, you can add your comment to the cell. To add a comment to cell B1, do the following:

- Click inside cell B1 on your spreadsheet.

- From the tabs on the Ribbon at the top of Excel, click on Review.

- Click on New Comment

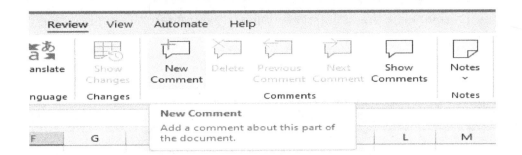

A textbox will appear to the right of cell B1, as in the image below:

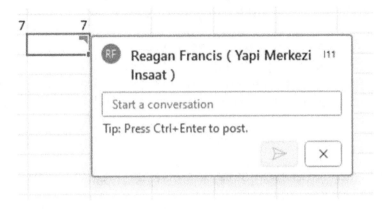

To add your comment, just start typing.

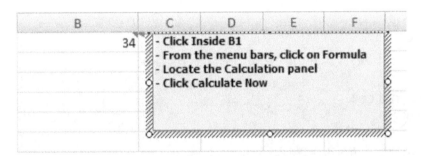

When you have finished typing your comment, click on any other cell. The comment will disappear. Notice that the cell now has a red triangle in the top right. This indicates that it contains a comment:

If you move your mouse pointer over cell B1 the comment will appear:

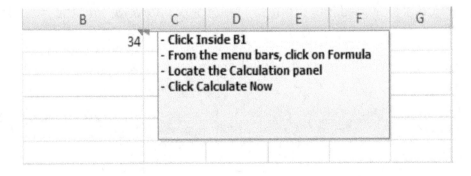

To get rid of a comment, right click the cell that contains the comment. Then, from the menu that appears, select Delete Comment.

2.14 FORMATTING

So far, we have not worried about getting everything to look neat and attractive, so that is what we are going to do now.
Unless you simply want to make a little simple calculation for yourself, you should consider the formatting of the spreadsheet.
If you need to make a large, complex spreadsheet that other people are going to use, you should be aware that, while the construction might appear logical to you, it can be difficult for others to understand the logic.
Appropriate formatting also indicates quality and credibility.
There is a myriad of options for formatting in Excel.
You can change row and column sizes, font types and sizes, colors, number formats, etc. You can even format the cells so that they change color depending on their value!

Text and colors

You are free to format text and numbers in cells and give them colors. You can format multiple cells at once if you make sure they are selected first.
Many functions in Excel can be found in several ways. The main ways to find a function are by means of the Ribbon, "contextual menus" or shortcut keys.

Formatting using the Ribbon.

Most features for text formatting are in the "Ribbon". Let us practice a little.

1. Try typing your name in a cell.
2. Ensure the cell is active.

The Ribbon is organized into different Tabs.
You need the tab labeled "Home", where you find the formatting functions.

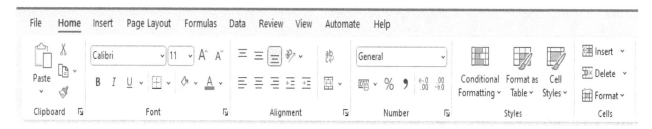

The buttons in the Ribbon are divided into groups. The group where we find the most important buttons is "Font" group.

3. Click on the button shown then the text will likely become red.

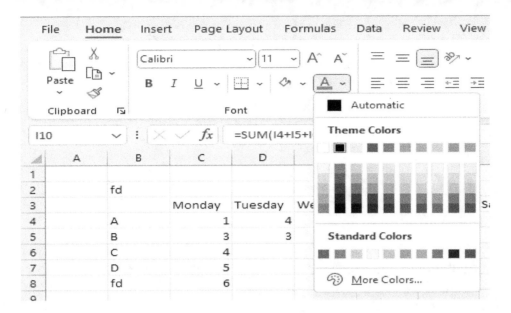

If you have played around with it previously, the text may get a different color, since there are several possibilities.

This button has a little arrow on the right-side giving access to more options.

4. Try clicking on the small arrow on the button. This gives you the opportunity to choose between several colors. Click on one of the blue hues. Your text is now blue.

You can also format multiple cells at once.

5. Highlight the cell with your name plus some more cells.

6. Click on the button in the Ribbon. Now you have a yellow background. Just as with the text, you could also have chosen a different color.

7. If you are still not satisfied, you can click on More Colors, and choose from up to 16 million different colors. That should be enough for most people.

8. Click the little arrow on the right button. This button is what we call the "Font Changer". Your font changer might display another font than "Calibri", but you do not risk ruining anything by clicking on it anyway!

9. You are about to select another font, so try, for example" Arial Black".

10. To the right of the font changer there is a button where you select the font size. Try for example 24. That will make the text much larger.

Try some of the other buttons to discover their effect.

Formatting using the shortcut menu.

Modern Windows programs rely largely on the shortcut menus that pop up when you click on something with your right mouse button. In the shortcut menu you find the most frequently used functions related to what you have just clicked on.

1. Type you name in a cell and press ENTER.
2. Click on the cell with the right mouse button to display the" shortcut menu".

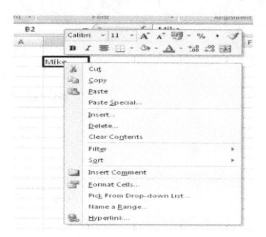

At the top of the shortcut menu, you will find buttons that resemble those in the Ribbon; they also work just the same way. But we must try some new features.

3. Click on the menu item Format Cells.

This will give you access to all the options available to format one or more cells. A dialog box opens, and you can choose between different Tabs at the top.

4. Select the Font tab and the following window appears:

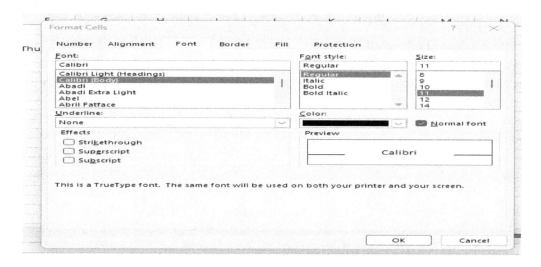

5. Select the font size and color that suits you, then click the Fill Tab. You can choose to fill the cell with a fill color, a pattern, or a color effect. We have already tried a normal fill color, so let us try something with effects!

6. Click on the Effects button and a new window will open.

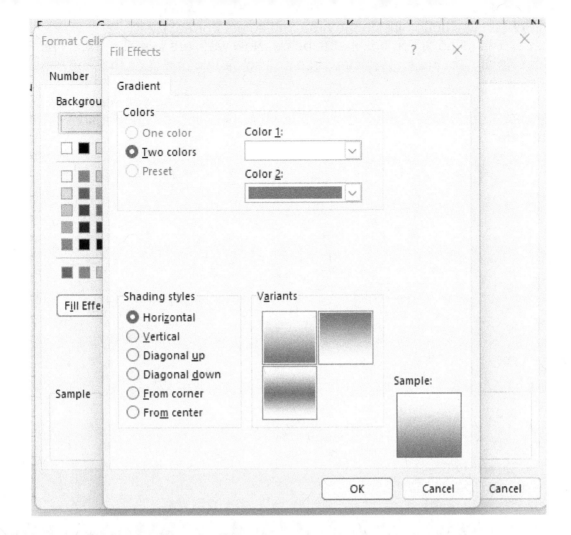

In Excel the effect colors consist of two colors which gradually blend into each other.
7. Try choosing colors by clicking on Color 1 and Color 2.
8. Try clicking on the different Shading Types. When you are satisfied, click OK.
9.Click OK again. My little experiment turned out thus:

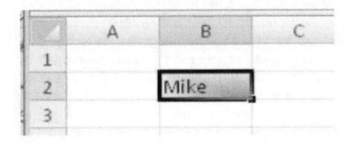

Borders and Frames

When you look at a blank worksheet, there are some thin lines that indicate where the cells are. Without these lines it would be harder to identify a particular cell in the sheet.
But these "grid lines" are only auxiliary lines; they are not written out unless you specifically request it, and if you provide some cells with a fill color, grid lines will not be displayed in that area. But you can add borders and frames yourself, and you can even choose the color and how thick they should be.

1. Select cell region B2:E5.

2. Click with the right mouse button inside the area and select Format Cells.

3. Select the Border Tab in the dialog box that appears. Now we need to make some grid lines. We would like to have a thick border around the selected area and some thin grid lines that show the cells inside the area.

It is actually very easy to do, but it is quite difficult to explain because you must click in many different places in the correct order. I have therefore made the following illustration that shows what you need to click and in what order.

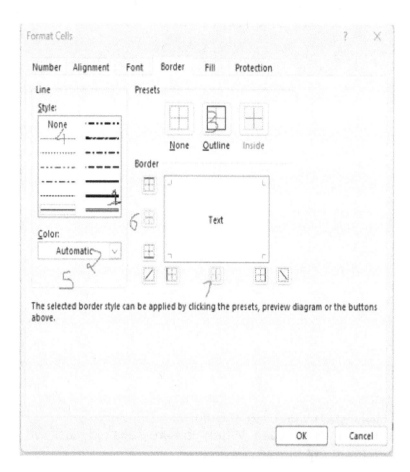

The window is divided into three groups of objects you can click on. The first group is "Line" where you choose how your edges should look and what color they should have.

The next group is the "Presets", where you can choose between None, Contour, and Interior.

The function none is relevant if you have already made some lines that you want removed. The Contour function makes a frame around the selected cell region with the line you have chosen. The Interior function draws lines inside the selected cell regions, which highlights the individual cell. The final group in the dialog box is "Border", where you can do the same thing as in the group "Presets".

The difference is that here you can control exactly which lines you want. For example, you can settle for a thick line at the top and bottom of the marked area or you can choose to have only horizontal interior lines. Let us see how it works. We will follow the numbering in figure above.

1. First, click the thick line.
2. Choose a color
3. Click on Contour.

You have now defined the frame around the selected area.

4. Click on the thin line.

5. Choose a color as in point 2, but preferably a second color for illustration
6. Click on the button for interior horizontal lines. If you wish, you can choose another line type and color before you proceed to point 7.
7. Click OK. Your result hopefully looks like mine in Figure below.

Now you should have a good insight into the possibilities for coloring your worksheet. Colors can have a large impact. If used right, they can make a complicated spreadsheet much more logical, simple, and inviting. I use formatting for larger spreadsheets, although I may be the only one who needs them. For example, I almost always color cells with formulas, while I keep cells without formulas white.
In this way I can quickly see which numbers the ones are being entered and which are the calculated values.

Number Formats

We will now leave the department of colors and stripes and return to numbers. Numbers can be displayed in many ways. Which of the following numbers do you think is most readable?
1000000 or 1.000.000
If the figure referred to money, one million could also be written as "kr 1,000,000.00.
In other cases, you might be interested in controlling how many decimal places to display. This you also control via formatting.

1. Type the following number 123456 in cell B2.
2. Click with the right mouse button on the cell and choose Format Cells.
3. Click on the Number Tab if it has not been selected already. Now we can choose between a lot of different number formats. In the pane "Category" you can choose between the basic types, and depending on what you choose, different options will appear.
Try clicking on the different types, so you get an idea of the possibilities before we proceed.
Do not click OK.
Click on the category Number, which will make the dialog box look like figure below.

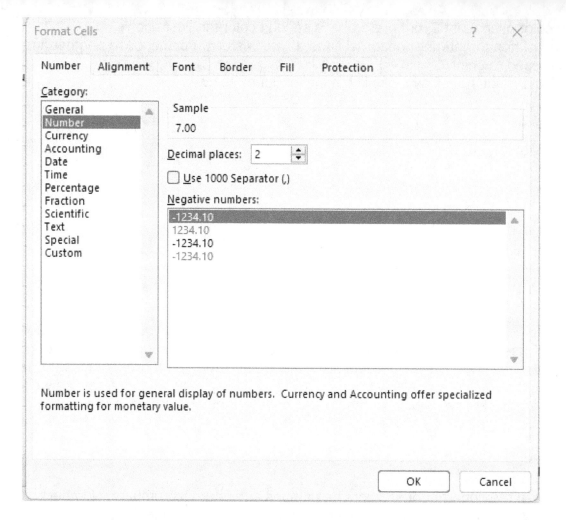

4. At Number Of Decimal Places, choose "1".
5. Put a check mark by Use Thousands Separator. This means that periods are inserted in the number, like the example with 1.000.000 instead of 1000000.
6. Click OK.

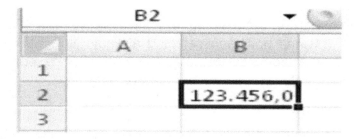

Now your number looks like Figure above. The figure remains the same, but it appears in a different way. Please note that, although only one decimal place is displayed, all decimals are still counted.
You will see that if you look at the formula bar when the cell is selected.
Number formats have no bearing on the cell value.

7. Type 25%in cell B4 and press ENTER.
In this case Excel assists a little with the number format because it displays "25%". What you are not able to see is that the cell's value is 0.25. You can discover that by changing the number format to a number with two decimal places.
If you wish, you can try it.

Date and Time

You can write the date and/or time in several ways. When you type a date and/or time, Excel automatically formats the cell to an appropriate date or time format. All you have to do is type it in correctly. Dates will be recognized if you write them in one of the following ways:
25 -3-2008
or
25/3/2008
Times will be recognized if you write them in one of the following ways:
17:45
(hours: minutes)
17:45:30
(hours: minutes: seconds).
Date and time can of course also be combined by putting spaces in between, for example:
25 -03 -2008 17:45:30
You can perform calculations with dates and times. Excel uses a clever numbering system to keep track of dates and times.
When there is a date and/or time in a cell, the cell just has a numerical value that is formatted as date/time.
This could lead to headaches if it were to be used in a calculation, but it is simple.
Excel's calendar begins on January 1, 1900, 00.00.
This time point has the value "1". January 2, 1900, 00:00,
has the value "2".
In other words, For each day 1 is added.
The time is also part of this system, so January 2, 1900, at 12.00 noon, has the value "2.5". One hour thus corresponds to 1/24, or 0.041666667 to be precise.
Excel operates with 10 decimal places, so you can calculate with very accurate time points.

Formatting Tables

When working with a spreadsheet, one usually makes tables. Once you have made a table where you have inserted sum formulas, etc., Excel can format the table automatically, so it looks neat and presentable.

	C4		f_x	750		
	A	B	C	D	E	F
1						
2			January	February	March	
3		Turnover	1000	1200	950	
4		Costs	750	800	780	
5		Surplus	250	400	170	
6						

1. Create a table like the one in figure above.
2. Ensure that one of the cells in the table is the active one.
3. In the Ribbon, make sure that the" Home" Tab has been selected. Then Click on the Format As Table button in the Ribbon.

Format
as Table ▾
Styles

4. A menu will pop up and you can choose a table layout
5. A small box will appear and ask what region you wish to define as the table. It is usually right on target if you have done as I have shown.
6. Finally you must also make sure to put a marker in the My Table Has Headers box, which ensures that the column headers are highlighted.
7. Click OK.

Now your table should have been formatted with the highlighted title and everything. You can still change the formatting of individual cells if you like.

My table came to look like this:

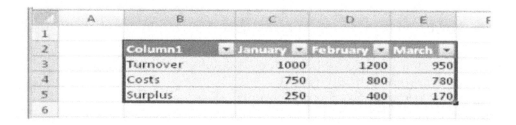

But formatting of the table is not the only thing that has happened. In addition to formatting the table, the Ribbon at the top has changed, and you now see a range of functions that relate to the tables.

A Tab has been added in the Ribbon, which is available when you activate a cell in the table.

That is because the tables in Excel are not only about the formatting. There are some special options when you define specific areas of a worksheet as tables, which we will return to later in the book.

But it is not the only thing that has happened; some arrows have appeared beside the column headers.

These arrows can be used as "filters", where you can select specific data that you want to see. It has no relevance to a table like the one we just created, but if you work with a table with many data covering hundreds of lines it can be very practical.

If you print the worksheet, the arrows do not show on the printout, but you can also remove the arrows by disabling the filter. To disable the filter, do as follows:

1. Select the Data Tab in the Ribbon.
2. Click on the Filter button. It is easy to find because at present the filter is active, which means the button is highlighted with a red/orange color.

Column1	January	February	March
Turnover	1000	1200	950

Filter

Sort & Filt.

Now the arrows have disappeared from the column headers, but there has also been another change in the table.

In the upper left corner, it suddenly says "column1", when you define a field as a table Excel requires that all columns have a header.

This is because Excel will use the headlines in connection with the sorting and filtering features that are available for tables.

This is also the reason you cannot delete the text. You can write anything you want, but Excel does not allow this cell to be empty. I you want it to be empty anyway, I have a little" trick" for you.

1. Activate the cell.
2. Press the spacebar on the keyboard.
3. Press the ENTER key on your keyboard

Now you have typed an empty space in the cell, and spaces are invisible.

Conditional Formatting

Excel can change the color, font, etc. of a cell, depending on what value it has. You can pre-select a number format that shows negative numbers in red, but conditional formatting gives more options.

The way it works is that you give a cell the format you would like it to have as a starting point.

Then you set up a list of the alternative formats it can have, and what conditions must be met for it to change the format.

Imagine an example where you want to build up statistics on absenteeism rates among a group of employees.

You make a list of employees and a calculation of absence rates. If the absence rate for the individual employee is less than 5%, the cell should have default formatting.

If absence rates are greater than 5% but less than 8%, the cell should be marked with a yellow background color.

If the absenteeism rate is 8% or more, the cell should have white writing on a red background color.

If you have worked with conditional formatting in earlier versions of Excel, this may not be new to you. In addition, it has become possible to use a value-dependent color spectrum, which can give quite impressive results.

	A	B	C	D	E	
1						
2		1	6	11	16	
3		2	7	12	17	
4		3	8	13	18	
5		4	9	14	19	
6		5	10	15	20	
7						
8						

E7

Let us try a couple of exercises.

1. Create a spreadsheet as in Figure above.
2. Select the cell region B2: E6. The selected cells will be included in the conditional formatting.
3. Ensure that the "Home" Tab has been selected in the Ribbon and click the Conditioned Formatting button.

Conditional
Formatting ▾

4. In the menu that appears, point to "Top/Bottom Rules" to make a submenu appear.
5. Click on Top 10%. This means that those 10% of the cells that have the highest values will be highlighted.
You will now fine-tune the formatting. A dialog box will appear where you can change the rate distribution. For example, you might want to highlight the cells with the top 20% values. You also can choose between several predefined formatting by clicking on the list in the dialog box.
If you select Custom Format on the list, you can fine-tune the format and choose exactly what colors you want.
6. Select Light Red Fill With Dark Red Text.
7. Click OK.
Now the cells with the two highest values should be selected. In my case it looks like this:

	A	B	C	D	E	F
1						
2		1	6	11	16	
3		2	7	12	17	
4		3	8	13	18	
5		4	9	14	19	
6		5	10	15	20	
7						

Figure below with Conditioned formatting where the top 20% values have been highlighted:

	A	B	C	D	E
1					
2		1	6	11	16
3		2	21	12	17
4		3	8	13	18
5		4	9	14	19
6		5	10	15	20
7					

8. Try typing the number 21 in the cell with the value 7.
This will make the highlight disappear from the cell with the value 19, because now the cells with the values 20 and 21 constitute the top 10%.

9. Select all the cells again.
10. Select the Conditioned Formatting button again.
11. Point to Highlight Cell Rules to make a submenu appear.
12. Click on Between, which gives us the opportunity to highlight cells with values within a certain range.
13. In the dialog box that appears, write 15 in the first field and 20 in the second field.
14. Choose the format Yellow Fill With Dark Yellow Text.
15. Click OK.

Now you have two different conditional formatting that work in the same cells.
First, the top 10% of cells are colored pink, and then the cells with values between 15 and 20 are colored yellow. The conditions operate in the order you created them.
It was the yellow formatting that was created last, therefore the cell with the value 20 is also yellow, although it was previously pink.

16. Ensure the cell region we have been working with so far is selected.
17. Click on the Conditioned Formatting button again.
18. Choose the menu item Manage Rules in the menu that appears.

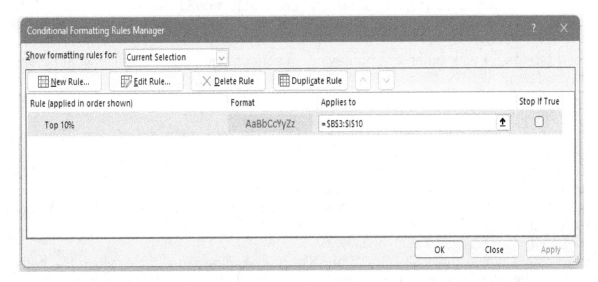

You now could manage the order of the rules you have set up for conditional formatting.
You can also add, delete, or modify rules. In this exercise we just need to reverse the order.

19. Ensure that the rule for Cell Value between 15 and 20 has been chosen.
20. Click on the Move Down button.
21. Click OK.

Now your spreadsheet looks like this:

	A	B	C	D	E
1					
2		1	6	11	16
3		2	21	12	17
4		3	8	13	18
5		4	9	14	19
6		5	10	15	20
7					

Now the rule is applied to highlight the top 10% values last, so cell E6 has become pink again.
There are many other possibilities for conditional formatting.
It is, for example, possible to give the cell a hue from pale yellow to deep red, depending on how high the value is.
Many of these options arguably belong to the "extra icing on the cake" category, but they can also be used to make the spreadsheet more readable.

Themes and Styles

Themes and Styles is a new option in Excel, but you probably recognize Styles from Word and Power Point, where they have been used in many earlier versions.
Use of Themes and Styles helps you make "nice" worksheets where you can easily create a uniform and neat appearance.
As you might have noticed by now, I like to emphasize that the spreadsheet should do more than just calculate correctly.
If you are building large and complicated spreadsheets to be used by anyone other than yourself, it is important that it is logical and clearly structured, and preferably nice to look at.
When it is neat and easy to understand, there will not be so many mistakes. It will also make it more credible.
If you got good grades for your arithmetic homework in school, you probably know what I mean. If you did not get good grades, it might be a consolation that Excel now can assist you.
Themes can be regarded as an overarching set of guidelines for the fonts and color combinations you can use in your spreadsheet.
You can even define your own Themes, but Excel comes with many predefined Themes where the coolers already match nicely.
A Theme defines for example that all header cells must have green background color and be written in bold type, while cells with formulas should be bright green.
If you change the Theme for the entire worksheet, the changes will be reflected in all the cells to which you have assigned a "Style".
A style is something you assign to each cell.
You can for example define that cell B2, C2 and D2 are headings in a table, while the cells below are general number-cells. At the bottom you might have calculated a sum, in which case you can give the lower cells the style "Calculation". Let us see how it works.
1.Start with a blank spreadsheet and create a table as shown in figure below.
The table does not really make sense and is only meant as an example.

	A	B	C	D	E
1					
2			January	February	March
3		Monday	1	6	11
4		Tuesday	2	7	12
5		Wensday	3	8	13
6		Thursday	4	9	14
7		Friday	5	10	15
8		Sum	15	40	65
9					

We start by assigning a "theme" to the spreadsheet. This theme will affect our subsequent formatting of the spreadsheet.
2. Choose the Page Layout Tab in the Ribbon and click on the button furthest to the left, called Themes
3. A menu will appear where you can choose between various themes. Click on the Sequence theme.

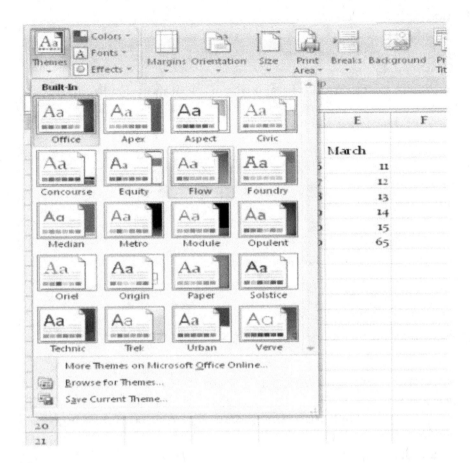

Now there are few visible changes in the spreadsheet. Only the font in the cells has changed.
4. Select the cell region C2:E2.
5. Choose Home Tab in the Ribbon and click on the Cell Styles button.

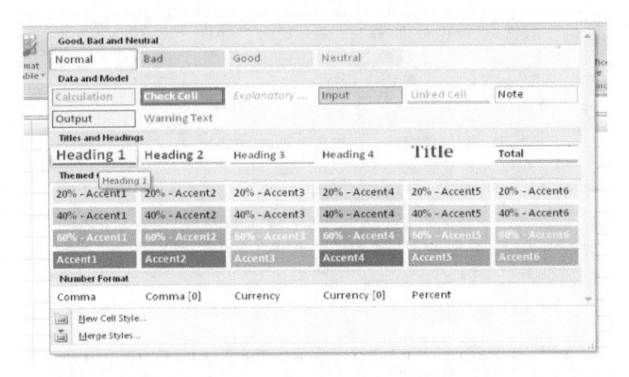

When you click the Cell Style button, a menu will appear where you can choose from a variety of named Styles. When you point to the individual Styles with your mouse, you can see how it will look in your table.

6. Click on the Style Heading 1.
7. Select cell region B3:B8.
8. Click the Cell Styles button and choose the style Accent1.
9. Select cell region C8:E8.
10. Click on the Cell Style button and choose the Calculation Style. If you have done as I, your spreadsheet will look like this:

	A	B	C	D	E	F	G
1							
2			January	Februa	March		
3		Monday	1	6	11		
4		Tuesday	2	7	12		
5		Wensday	3	8	13		
6		Thursday	4	9	14		
7		Friday	5	10	15		
8		Sum	15	40	65		
9							
10							

Now we will try some other colors, but we do not want to format the individual cells again so we will choose a different color theme.
Select the Page Layout Tab in the Ribbon, then click the Themes button Search.
Click on the theme metropolitan.
Now your spreadsheet looks like this:

	A	B	C	D	E
1					
2			Janua	Februa	March
3		Monday	1	6	11
4		Tuesday	2	7	12
5		Wensday	3	8	13
6		Thursday	4	9	14
7		Friday	5	10	15
8		Sum	15	40	65
9					

Now you have been introduced to Themes and Styles, and you can now experiment with them on your own.
If you continue working with Themes and Styles, you may also find that when you insert charts, graphs etc., they will also have colors defined in the color theme you have chosen, and so it all fits together.

PART THREE:

EXCEL CHARTS

3.1 HOW TO SORT DATA

Later, you'll see how to create a variety of charts and chart styles with Excel. If you've ever used previous versions of the software, you'll appreciate how easy it is to produce impressive results.
First, though, we'll tackle the subject of how to sort data. The two subjects are not really related, but the data going into our charts is a good opportunity to learn about this important topic.

Sorting Data

To make a start, you need to create the spreadsheet below. You don't need to use the same colors as ours, but reproduce the data and the headings exactly as they are in this one:

	A	B	C	D	E	F
1			Viewing Figures			
2						
3	BBC 1			ITV		
4		Millions			Millions	
5	National Lottery	6.27		Who...Millionare	10.99	
6	Ready Steady Cook	6.33		Heartbeat	10.22	
7	Vicar of Dibley	6.34		Bad Girls	7.42	
8	Ground Force	6.71		The Bill	6.54	
9	Holby City	6.99		The Vice	6.37	
10	Lenny Henry	7.03		Blind Date	6.31	
11	DIY SOS	7.2		Stars in their Eyes	6.26	
12	Changing Rooms	7.38		Footballer's Wives	6.17	
13	Antiques Roadshow	7.68		Champions League	6.09	
14	Casualty	8.82		Inspector Morse	5.81	
15						

Our spreadsheet is all about the viewing figures for the two main TV channels in the UK. The data is a bit old, but that's not important. If we have some nice information to sort, that's what matters.
The viewing figures for ITV have been sorted, from the highest first to the lowest last. The BBC1 figures are still waiting to be sorted. Let's see how to do that now.

Descending Sort

We want to sort the BBC1 viewing figures in the same way that the ITV figures have been sorted. We'll put the highest program first and the lowest last. This is called a Descending Sort. If you do it the other way round, it's known as an Ascending Sort.
The first thing to do is to highlight the information that you want to sort. In your spreadsheet, highlight cells A5 to B14. The crucial thing to remember when you want to sort data in Excel is to include the text as well as the numbers. If you don't, you'll end up with a spreadsheet where the numbers don't relate to the information, which could spell disaster in bigger spreadsheets!
Your highlighted spreadsheet, though, should look like this one:

	BBC 1	
3		
4		Millions
5	National Lottery	6.27
6	Ready Steady Cook	6.33
7	Vicar of Dibley	6.34
8	Ground Force	6.71
9	Holby City	6.99
10	Lenny Henry	7.03
11	DIY SOS	7.2
12	Changing Rooms	7.38
13	Antiques Roadshow	7.68
14	Casualty	8.82
15		

To sort your BBC 1 viewing figures, do the following:
- From the Excel tabs at the top of the screen, click Data:

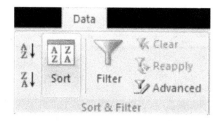

- From the Sort & Filter panel, click Sort.
- A dialogue box appears:

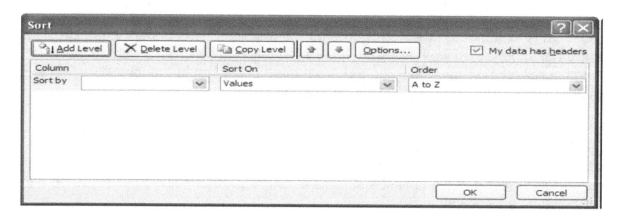

The Sort By drop-down list seems empty. Click the down arrow to reveal the columns you selected:

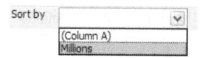

We want to sort this by the values in the Millions column. So, select Millions from the Sort by list. Sort On is OK for us - it has Values. But click to see the options in the drop-down list:

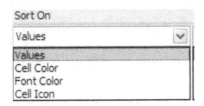

Values is the one you'll use the most. Once we have a Sort By and Sort On option selected, we can then move on to the Order.

Click the down arrow to see the options on the Order list:

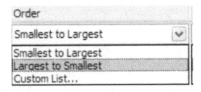

Select Largest to Smallest. Your Sort dialogue box should then look like this:

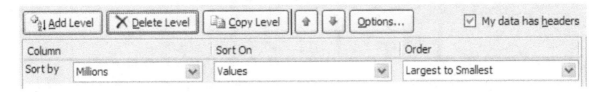

If you clicked OK, your data would be sorted. But the level buttons at the top can come in handy. If two items in your data have the same numbers, then you can specify what to sort by next. For example, if we have two program that have 6.3 million viewers, we could specify that the names of the program be sorted alphabetically.

To do this, click the Add Level button, and you'll see some additional choices appear. You'll see the same lists as the Sort By box. If you select Column A, and then Descending, Excel will do an alphabetical sort if two items have the same viewing figures.

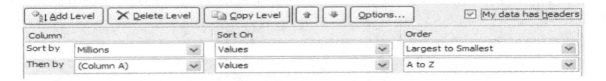

In the image above, we've added a "Then By" part, just in case there is a tie. You don't have to do this, as we have no numbers that are the same. Click OK to sort your data, though.

If everything went well, your sorted data should look like this:

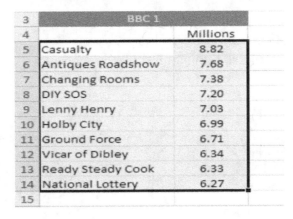

	BBC 1	
		Millions
Casualty		8.82
Antiques Roadshow		7.68
Changing Rooms		7.38
DIY SOS		7.20
Lenny Henry		7.03
Holby City		6.99
Ground Force		6.71
Vicar of Dibley		6.34
Ready Steady Cook		6.33
National Lottery		6.27

But that's all we need to do for the sort. You can move on to creating your first chart in Excel.

3.2 CREATE AN EXCEL CHART

We're now going to create a chart from our BBC1 Viewing figures. If you haven't yet completed the sorting tutorial, go back one page, and follow along with the lesson. You'll then have some sorted viewing figures to create a chart from.
When our chart is finished, though, it will look like this:

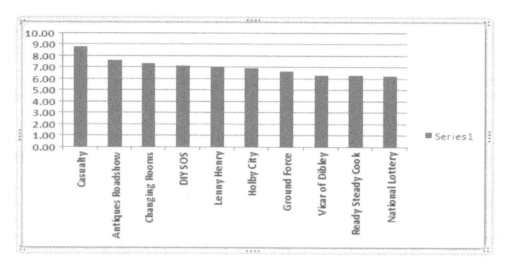

A little later, you'll see how to improve on this basic chart.
To start making your chart, highlight the BBC1 programmers, and the viewing figures. If you have just finished the sorting section, this data should still be highlighted, and look like this:

3	BBC 1	
4		Millions
5	Casualty	8.82
6	Antiques Roadshow	7.68
7	Changing Rooms	7.38
8	DIY SOS	7.20
9	Lenny Henry	7.03
10	Holby City	6.99
11	Ground Force	6.71
12	Vicar of Dibley	6.34
13	Ready Steady Cook	6.33
14	National Lottery	6.27
15		

With your program and the viewing figures highlighted, do this:
- From the tabs on the Excel Ribbon, click on Insert.
- Locate the Charts panel. It looks like this in Excel:

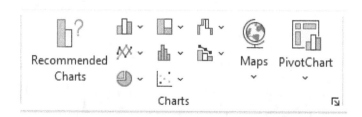

For this first one, we'll create a Column Chart. So, click the down arrow on the Column item of the Chart Panel. You'll see a list of available charts to choose from. Select the first one, the chart highlighted below (2D Column):

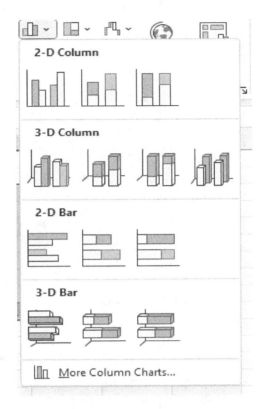

When you make your selection, a new chart appears on the same spreadsheet that you have open. The chart should look the same as the one at the top if this page.

But notice that the Excel Ribbon has changed. The design menu is selected, along with options for Chart Layouts:

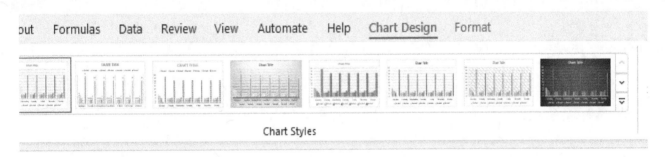

3.3 RESIZING AN EXCEL CHART

To resize your chart, do the following:
- Move your mouse pointer to the middle black square on the bottom row (if you can't see any black squares around your chart, click on the chart with the left mouse button to select it)
- Your mouse pointer will change to the shape of an arrow-headed line, like the one in the image below:

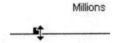

- When you mouse pointer changes to the shape above, hold down your left mouse button.
- Keep your left mouse button held down and drag downwards.

- Let go of the mouse button when the bottom of your chart reaches about Row 22
- Your chart should look like the one in the next picture:

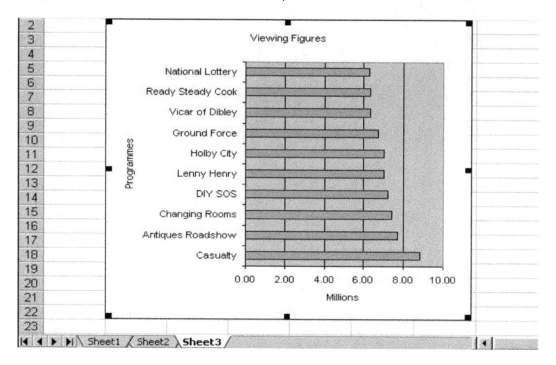

As you can see, all the programs are now showing. You can make your chart wider by moving your mouse over the right middle black square, and then dragging outwards. But careful not to drag too far out because some of your program will disappear. If this happens, click Edit from the menu bar, then click "Undo" from the menu.

We can make some of the Titles bold. To make your titles bold, do the following:
- Click on Viewing Figures but click with your right mouse button.
- A small menu pops up.
- Click on Format Chart Title

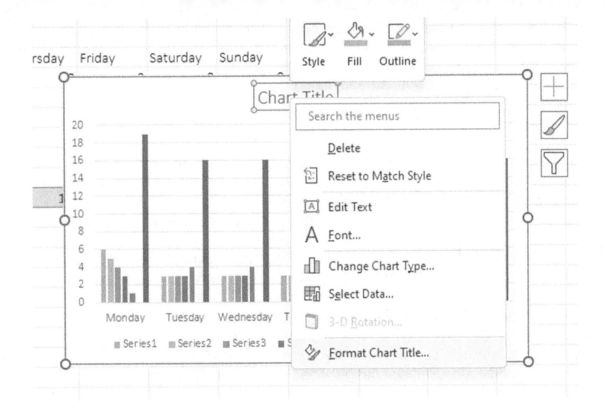

- Another dialogue box pops up.
- Select the Font tab strip.
- Choose a Bold font style and click the OK button.
- Your title is made Bold.
- Do the same with the program title and the Millions title.

Your Chart should now look something like the one below:

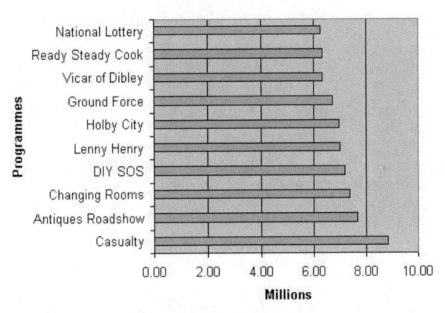

Except you might have noticed something. The program with the highest viewing figures, Casualty, is at the bottom. The program with the lowest viewing figures is at the top. We can do something about this quite easily. To get them other way around, do this:

- Click on Sheet 1 to return to your spreadsheet Data.
- Make sure the data is still highlighted.
- Click on Data from the menu bar.
- From the drop-down menu, click on Sort.
- On the Sort dialogue box, change the two Descending radio buttons to Ascending.
- Click the OK button.
- Click back on Sheet 2 to see your Chart.
- The Highest programs should now be at the top, and the lowest at the bottom.

The above method is not an ideal solution, but that is due to the nature of the Chart type we have chosen. We'll now do something different with the ITV programs. We'll create a different chart - a Pie Chart.

3.4 CHART STYLES AND CHART LAYOUTS

You can easily change the Style of your chart. If you can't see the Styles, click anywhere on your chart to select it, and you should see the Ribbon change. The Styles will look like this:

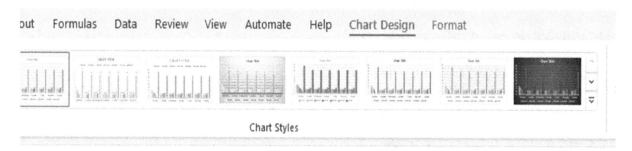

Click on any chart style, and your chart will change. To see more styles, click the arrows to the right of the Chart Styles panel:

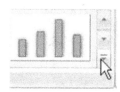

Chart Layouts

You can also change the layout of your chart in the same way. Locate the Chart Layout panel on the Design tab of the Excel Ribbon bar. It looks like this in Excel:

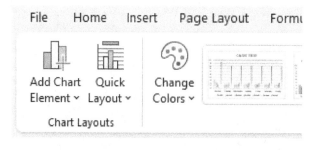

Again, click on each one in turn and see what happens to your chart. In the image below, we've gone for Layout 10:

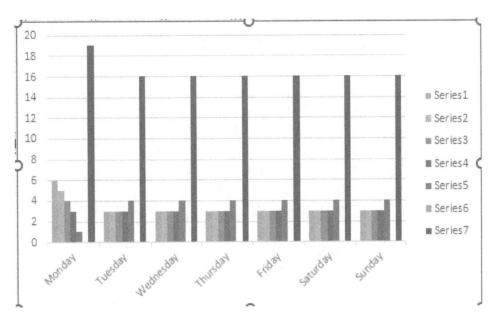

Changing the Chart Type - 2D Bar Charts

You can change the type of chart, as well. Instead of having a 2D column chart, as above, you can have a 2D bar chart. To change the chart type, locate the Type panel on the Excel Ribbon bar (you need to have your chart selected to see it):

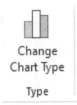

Change
Chart Type

Type

Then click Change Chart Type. You'll see a dialogue box appear. This one is from Excel:

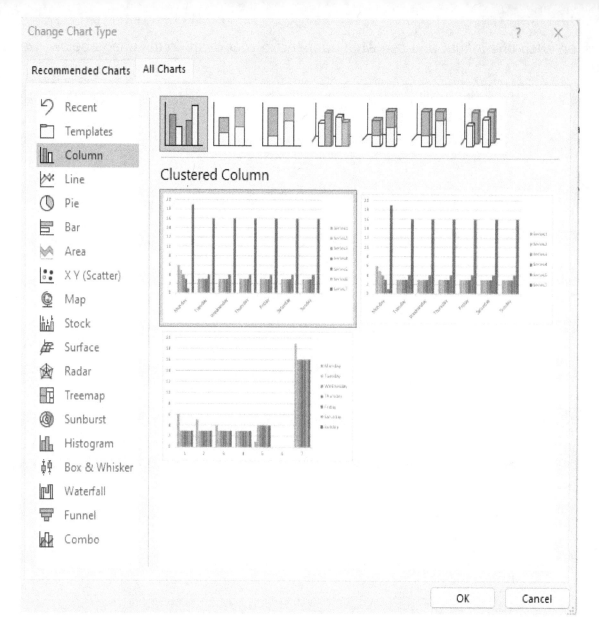

Select Bar from the list on the left of the dialogue box and click on the first Bar chart (Clustered Bar). Click OK to see your chart change:

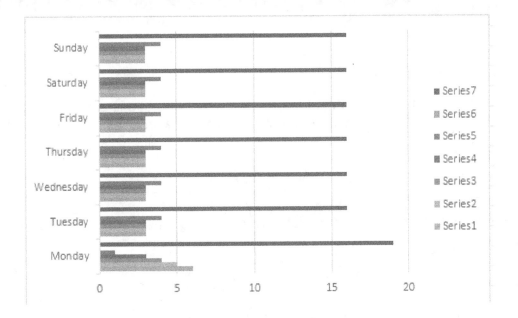

You can experiment with the types of charts in the dialogue box. But reset it to Bar chart, as above.

3.5 THE CHART TITLE AND SERIES TITLE

Your chart from the previous section should now look like this:

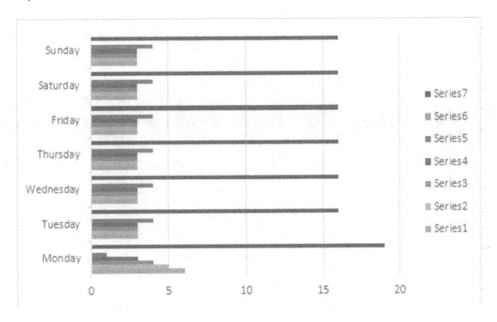

Once you have your chart in place, there are plenty of formatting options in Excel. In the chart above, for example, the title says, "Chart Title". And there's a not terribly descriptive orange square that says, "Series 1" (your bars may be blue). We'll see how to change that in a moment. But first, the Chart Title.

How to Change the Chart Title

To change the title of your chart, click on the title to select it:

The circles surrounding the title tell you that it is selected. Once the title is selected, click on the letter "C" of Chart. Hold your left mouse button down and highlight the two words, as in the image below:

Once your title is highlighted, you can change it by simply typing a new one:

While the title is highlighted, you can select a different font and font size, if you want (on the Home panel in the Excel Ribbon at the top.)
To deselect the title, click anywhere outside of it.

Formatting a Series Title

To change the Series 1 text on the Chart heading to something more descriptive, select the title as you did above:

Make sure the circles are there, and then right click. You should see the following menu appear in Excel:

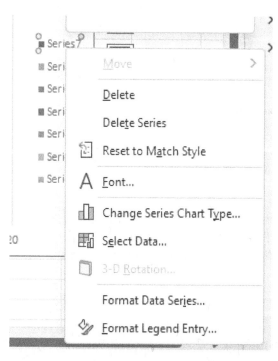

Click on "Select Data", you should then see the following dialogue box appear.

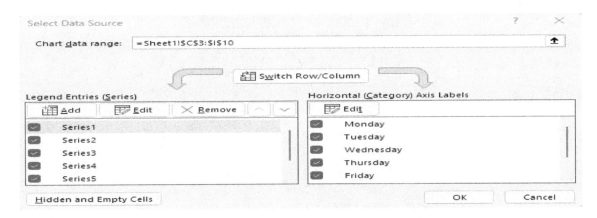

The Chart Data Range at the top of the dialogue box is highlighting the cells A5 to B14. This is the data we selected for the chart. Below this there is an area for Legend Entries (Series) and Horizontal Axis Labels. We'll see more of these later. For now, though, we just want to change Series 1 into something more descriptive.
So, click on Series 1 to highlight it. Then click the Edit button, as in the image below:

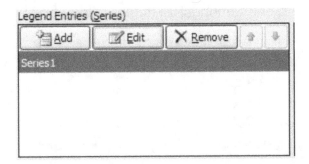

When you click the Edit button, you'll see a new dialogue box appear - Edit Series. It should look like this:

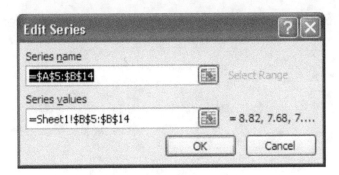

Notice the cells being referenced in the Series name area. They are cells A5 to B14. These same cells are also highlighted on the spreadsheet:

2		
3	BBC 1	
4		Millions
5	Casualty	8.82
6	Antiques Roadshow	7.68
7	Changing Rooms	7.38
8	DIY SOS	7.20
9	Lenny Henry	7.03
10	Holby City	6.99
11	Ground Force	6.71
12	Vicar of Dibley	6.34
13	Ready Steady Cook	6.33
14	National Lottery	6.27
15		
16		

Click on the BBC title instead, the one on Row 3 above. Your Edit Series dialogue box will have changed. The Series Name area will now say A3 (amongst all those dollars):

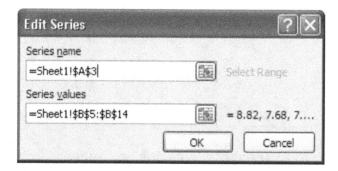

Click OK to get back to your Edit Data Source dialogue box. The Series legend will now say BBC:

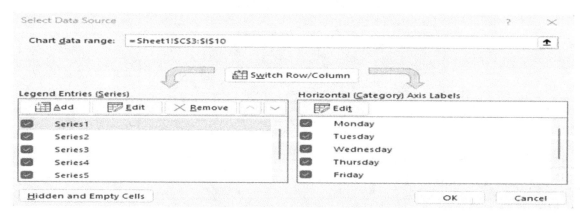

Click OK to return to your spreadsheet. But look what's happened to the chart. The Series 1 has gone. Next to the orange square, we now have BBC 1:

We'll meet these boxes again when we create a chart from scratch. For now, let's see some more formatting option you can do with an Excel chart.

3.6 THE CHART LAYOUT PANELS

In the previous part of this lesson on charts, you saw how to format a chart with various dialogue boxes. You can also format your charts using the menu items on the Excel Ribbon bar, at the top of the screen. With your chart selected, click the Layout menu. You should see this:

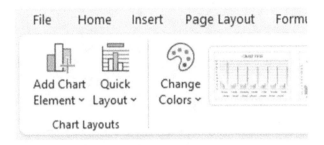

The Layout menu is a bit big for this page, so we've split it in two. But the chart Layout panel is split into several different sections and allows you to change the information in the chart.
For all versions of Excel, The first thing you may want to do is to give your chart a name.
To change the name of your chart, locate the Properties panel on the Layout menu:

Highlight the default name in the textbox and type a new one:

If you now click away from your chart, and then click back on it, you'll notice the name of the chart change:

The Add Chart Element

The Add chart element panel on the Layout menu lets you format the titles and legends on your chart. Here it is:

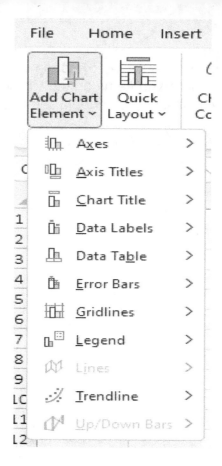

The first one is Chart Title. Click the arrow to see the options:

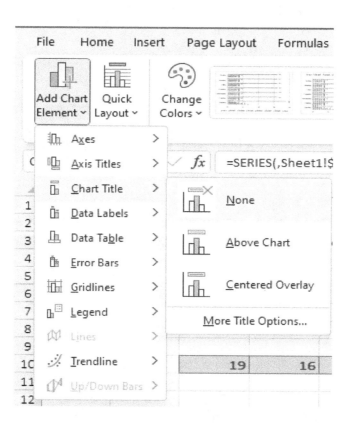

Click each item on the menu in turn to see what they do. Then click More Title Options. The following dialogue box will appear.

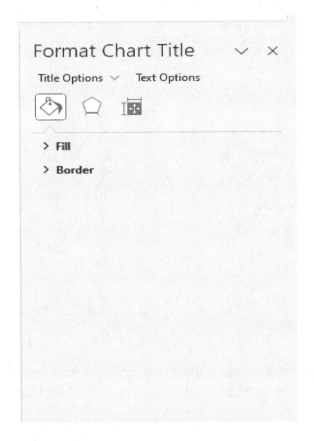

As you can see, there are options to change the Fill, Line, Line Style, Shadow, 3-D format, and Alignment. Play around with the options on the dialogue box to see what they do. The only thing you're changing here is the Chart Title. Click Close when you're done. If you don't like what you see, click the undo arrow at the top of Excel.

Change the Axis Title in Excel

The next item on the Add chart element panel is the Axis Title. Click the down arrow to see the options:

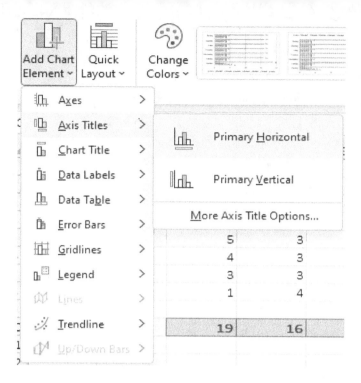

Now, our chart has no Axis Title. It just has numbers running across the bottom. Someone looking at the chart won't know what the numbers represent. Here's what our Chart looks like now:

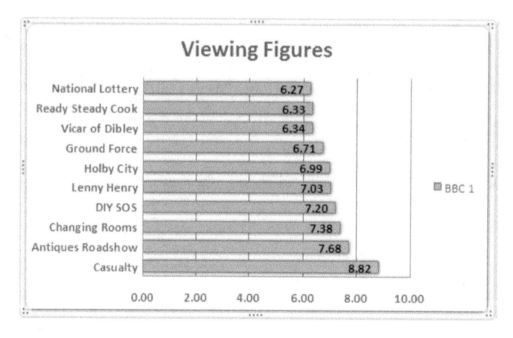

Chart Legend

The Chart's Legend is this one:
Now, our Legend is on the right of the chart. But you can move this. Click the Legend item on the Layout panel to see the various options:

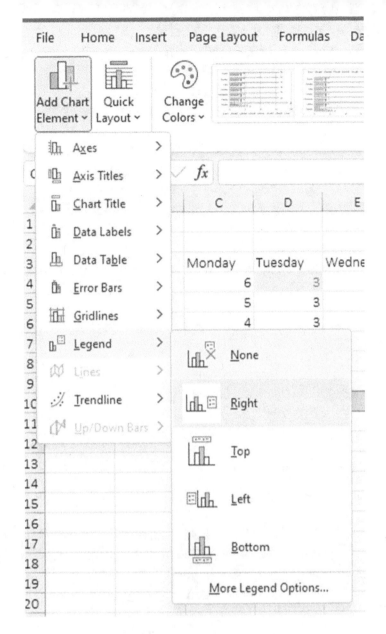

Click an option on the menu and watch what happens to your Legend. You should see it move around your chart.

Adding Data Labels to an Excel Chart

A Data Label is information overlaid on the chart bars. In our chart below, we have numbers overlaid on the orange bars:

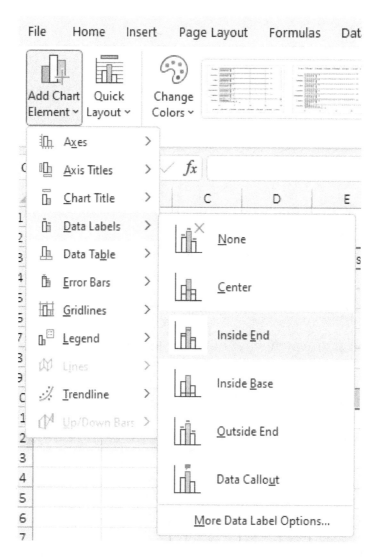

You can format these Data Labels. Click the Data Labels item on the Add Chart Element to see the following options:

The one what we have now is Inside Edge. Click on Outside End and your Data Labels will look like this:

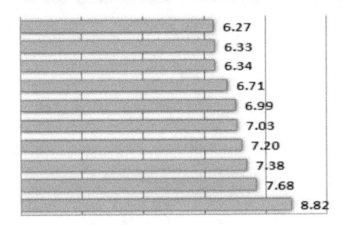

6.27
6.33
6.34
6.71
6.99
7.03
7.20
7.38
7.68
8.82

You can also see the options if you click More Data Label Options from the menu. You'll then see this dialogue box.

Again, play around with the options to see what they do. The first two, Label Options and Number, are the ones you'll probably use most often.

3.7 THE FORMAT CHART PANEL

In the previous lesson, you saw how to use the Layout panels to change the layout of the chart itself. The Format panels allow you to create some great looking charts with just a few mouse clicks.
Click on your chart to select it, and then click the Format menu at the top of the Excel Ribbon. You should see this long menu:

Using the various Format Panels on the Excel Ribbon, we'll format our chart from this:

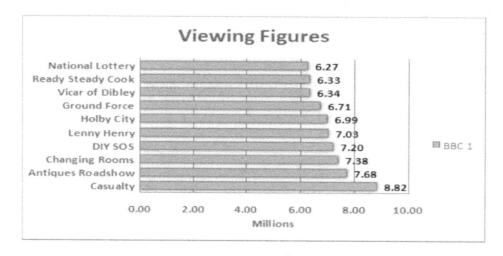

To this:

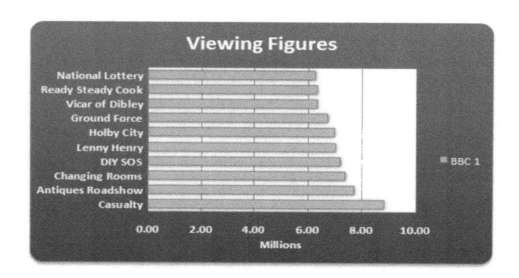

OK, it may look a bit gaudy! But at least it's lively. You can create a chart like this quite easily:
- First, click on your chart to highlight it.
- Click the Format menu on the Excel Ribbon
- Locate the Shape Styles panel:

Click the down arrow on the right of the panel to see the available styles.

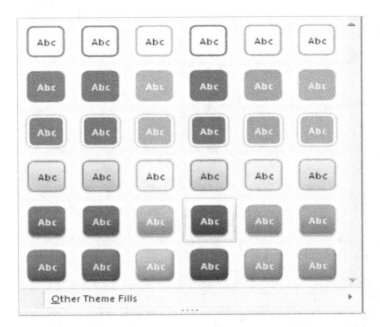

When you move your mouse over a style, your chart will change automatically. But you won't be able to see the full effect until you click away from the chart. We went for Style 28, the one that's highlighted in the image above. You get the rounded corners, the drop shadow, and the color fill.

Create your own Chart Style in Excel

You can create all that yourself, though. If you want to create your own style, try the following:
Fill your chart with a color by clicking the down arrow on Shape Fill on the Shape Styles panel.

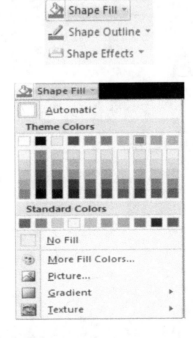

Select a color from the list. Or click "More Fill Colors". Once your chart has a color, you can liven it up a bit.
Still on the same menu, click on Gradient. The sub menu appears.

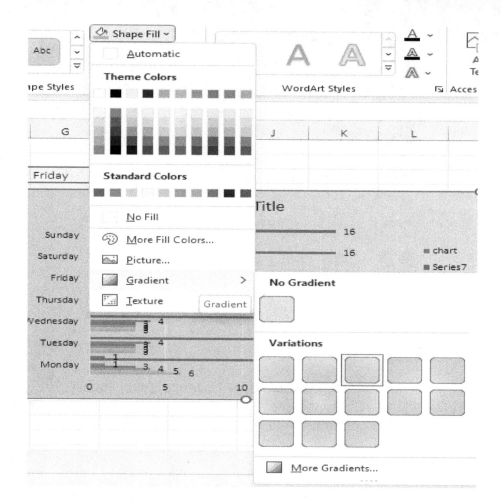

We went for one of the Dark Variations.
Next, you can spruce up the text on your chart. Locate the WordArt Styles panel:

Click the Text Fill button to see the available colors:

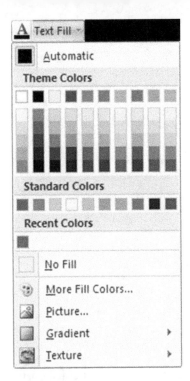

Once you have the chart background and text formatted the way you want it, you can add some rounded corners, and a bit of drop shadow. You can apply both of those from the Format Chart Area dialogue box. Here's how.

To bring up the Format Chart Area dialogue box, click the Format Selection button on the Current Selection panel:

You'll then see the following dialogue box appear.

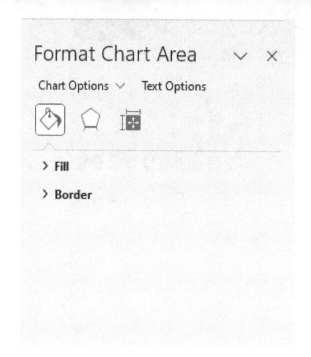

To get rounded corners, click Border. You'll then see the following options:

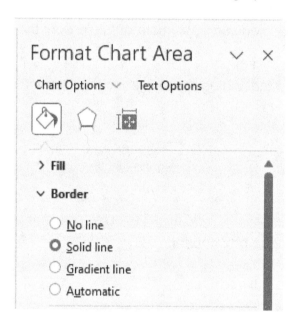

3.8 EXCEL PIE CHARTS

How to Create a Pie Chart in Excel

Pie charts are quite easy to create in Excel. In case you're not sure what a Pie Chart is, here's the basic one you'll be creating. Later, you'll add some formatting to this:

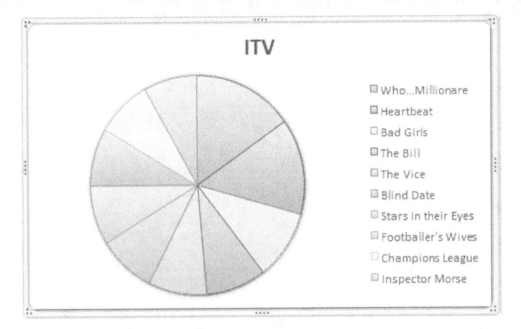

To make a start, you need to highlight some data. If you've been following along with the previous study, then you'll have some viewing figures data. You've created a 2D chart with the BBC data. This time we'll use the ITV data. If you don't have this data, create the following simple spreadsheet. The cells to use are D4 to E14:

	ITV
Who...Millionare	10.99
Heartbeat	10.22
Bad Girls	7.42
The Bill	6.54
The Vice	6.37
Blind Date	6.31
Stars in their Eyes	6.26
Footballer's Wives	6.17
Champions League	6.09
Inspector Morse	5.81

- Click inside cell E4 and change "Millions" to ITV if you already have the data from a previous lesson.
- Highlight the cells D4 to E14
- Click the Insert menu at the top of Excel.
- Locate the Chart panel, and the Pie item:

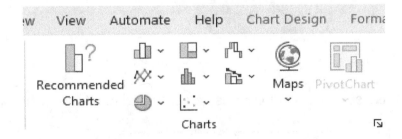

Click the down arrow and select the first Pie chart:

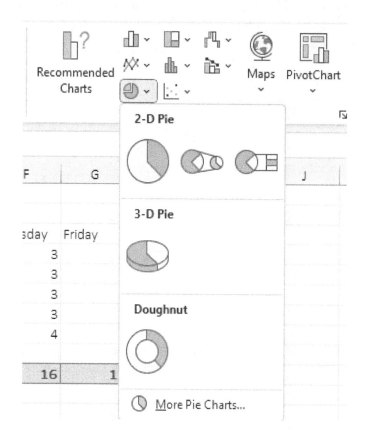

- A new Pie chart is inserted.
- Move your new pie chart by dragging it to a new location.
- Notice how all the segments of the pie chart are the same color in Excel:

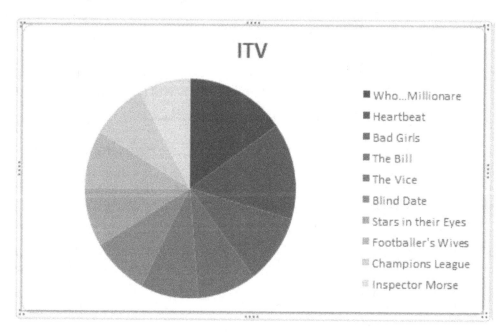

To get different colors, make sure that your chart is selected and locate the Chart Style panel:

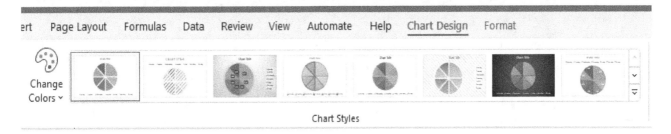

Click the down arrow to the right of the Chart Style panel to reveal the available styles.

We've gone for the second one, Style two. The chart will then look like this (your labels may well be at the bottom, though, depending on which version of Excel you have):

ITV

☐ Who...Millionare
☐ Heartbeat
☐ Bad Girls
☐ The Bill
☐ The Vice
☐ Blind Date
☐ Stars in their Eyes
☐ Footballer's Wives
☐ Champions League
☐ Inspector Morse

3.9 ADD DATA LABELS TO A PIE CHART

Now, though, there's no information about what each segment represents. We're going to add the numbers from our ITV viewing figures. These ones:

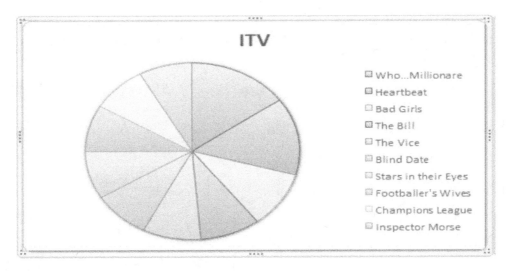

	ITV
Who...Millionare	10.99
Heartbeat	10.22
Bad Girls	7.42
The Bill	6.54
The Vice	6.37
Blind Date	6.31
Stars in their Eyes	6.26
Footballer's Wives	6.17
Champions League	6.09
Inspector Morse	5.81

To add the numbers from our E column (the viewing figures), left click on the pie chart itself to select it:

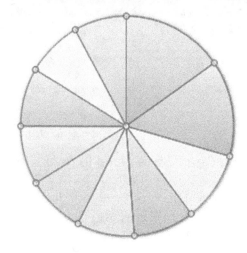

The chart is selected when you can see all those blue circles surrounding it. Now right click the chart. You should get the following menu:

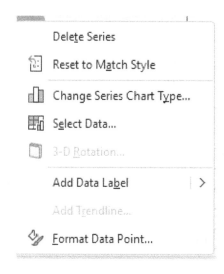

From the menu, select Add Data Labels. New data labels will then appear on your chart:

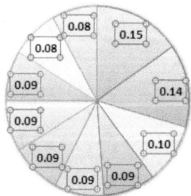

The values are in percentages. To change this, right click your chart again. From the menu, select Format Data Labels:

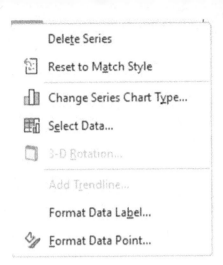

When you click Format Data Labels, you should get a dialogue box. This one:

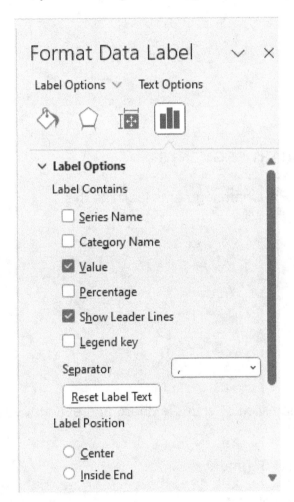

If there's a tick in Percentage, untick this and select Value:

Your chart will then have the correct numbers:

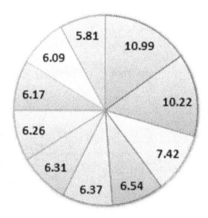

3.10 HOW TO FORMAT PIE CHART SEGMENTS

From the previous lesson, your Pie Chart segments look like this:

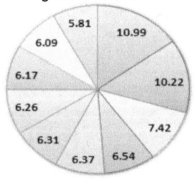

You can change the color of each slice of your pie chart, and even move a slice. Let's change the colors first.

Change the Color of a Pie Chart Segment

Left click on the pie chart itself to select it:

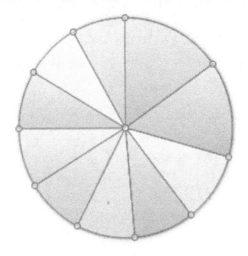

It is selected when you can see those round handles. Now left click on one of the segments to select just that individual slice. It's a little bit tricky, but if you do it right your pie chart should look like this:

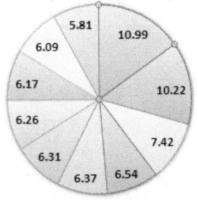

In the image above, only the 10.99 segment is selected. You should see round circles surrounding just that segment. Now right click your segment and, from the menu that appears, select Format Data Point:

You should see the following dialogue box appears:

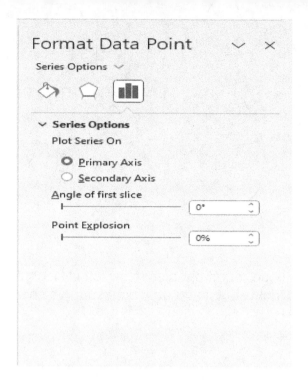

Click on Fill from the options on the left. The dialogue box changes to this:

There are quite a lot of options to experiment with. But select the Solid Fill option:

Fill

○ No fill
◉ Solid fill
○ Gradient fill
○ Picture or texture fill
○ Background

☑ Vary colors by slice

Color: 🎨 ▼

Transparency: |——————| 0% ▲▼

Now click the color picker, and choose a new color for the segment:

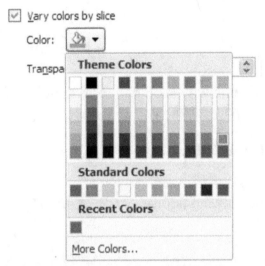

We've gone for a dark orange color but select any color you like.

Move a Pie Chart Segment in Excel

To move the slice that you've just colored, click back on Series Options.
Now click the Close button. Your chart should look something like this one:

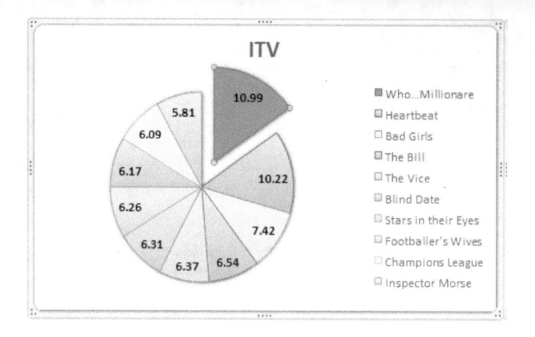

Change the rest of the slices in the same way. You can format the rest of the chart exactly like you did for the Bar chart. But it looks quite impressive as it is!

3.11 CREATE A 2D LINE CHART IN EXCEL

For this last chart, we'll compare the viewing figures of BBC1 and ITV. A line chart is better for this type of data. The chart we'll create looks like this:

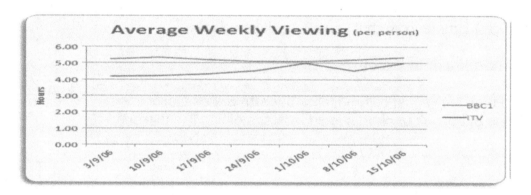

We're comparing how many hours per week a person watches BBC1 with how many hours they watch ITV. You'll need some data, of course. Start a new spreadsheet and enter the same data as below:

	A	B	C	D	E	F	G	H
1		Average Weekly Viewing (Hrs.Mins per person 15/10/06 to 3/09/06)						
2								
3		3/9/06	10/9/06	17/9/06	24/9/06	1/10/06	8/10/06	15/10/06
4	BBC1	5.27	5.37	5.23	5.13	5.12	5.21	5.37
5	ITV	4.19	4.23	4.33	4.54	5.00	4.57	5.01
6								

Once you have your spreadsheet data, highlight the cells A3 to H5. Now click Insert from the Excel Ribbon bar. Locate the Charts panel and click on Recommends Charts. From the dialogue box, select All Chart:

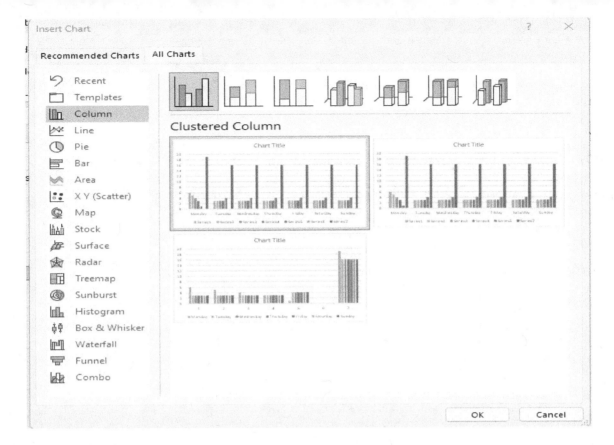

From the dialogue box, the left-hand side shows all the chart templates. Click on Line. Select the first Line chart, the one highlighted in the image above. Click OK and Excel will insert your chart. It should look like this:

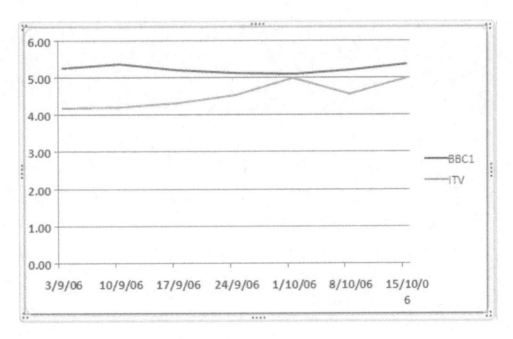

The chart looks a bit plain, now. You can change the color of the lines for BBC and ITV. Locate the Chart Styles panel on the Design menu:

Chart Styles

Click the down arrow on the right of the Chart Styles panel to reveal the available styles.

We've gone for the first one, top left. When you select a style, your chart will change:

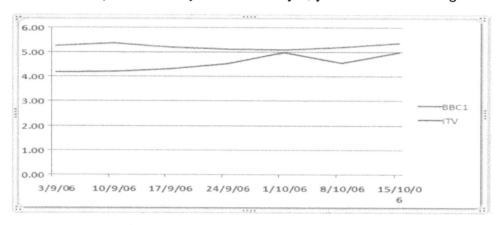

3.12 FORMAT AXIS TITLES

From the previous lesson, your 2D Excel Line Chart should look like this:

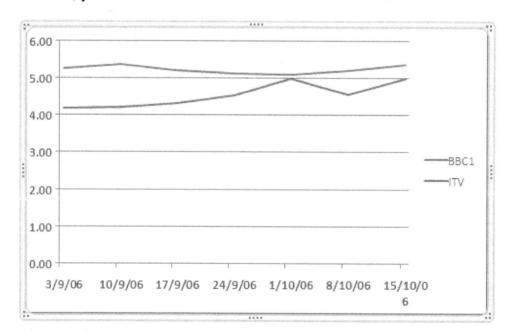

To format the dates on the bottom Axis, click on them with your left mouse button. With the dates Axis selected, right click. You should see this menu:

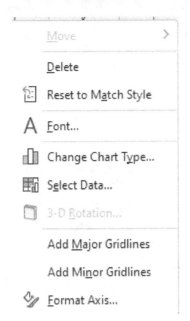

Select Format Axis from the menu, and you'll see the following dialogue box appear:

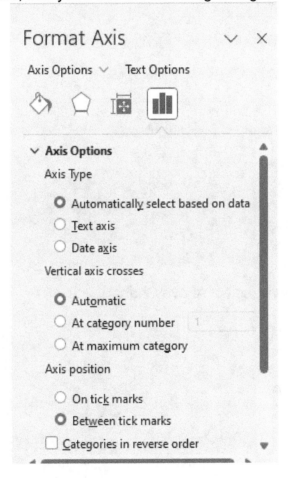

Under Axis Type, select Text Axis:

Axis Type:
- ○ Automatically select based on data
- ◉ Text axis
- ○ Date axis

Your dates should end up in the middle.

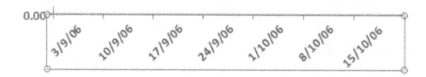

Adding an Axis Title

To add an Axis label at the top of your chart, click the Add Chart Element at the top of Excel:

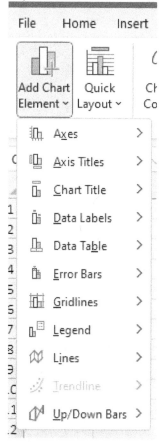

Click on Chart Title. From the menu, select Above Chart:

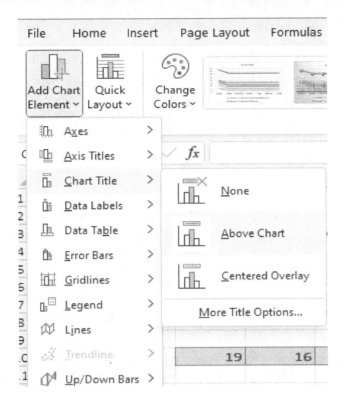

Add a Left Axis

We now need to add an Axis for the numbers running up the left of the chart. The numbers are the hours per week that people watch each channel - 0 to 6.

From the Add Chart Element menu still, select Axis Titles > Primary Vertical Axis Title:

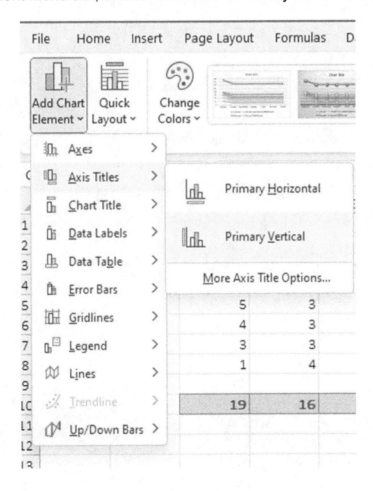

This will add a title like the following one:

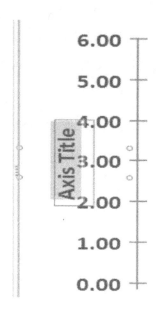

Highlight the default title and type Hours. You can move the title to the left by clicking and dragging. This is a little tricky, though! Use the Zoom tool at the bottom of Excel to zoom in on your target:

Move the Axis in to position:

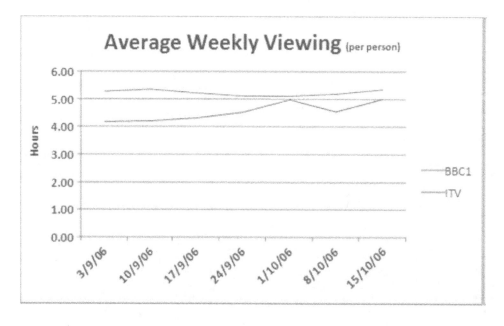

When you're done, your chart should now look like this one:

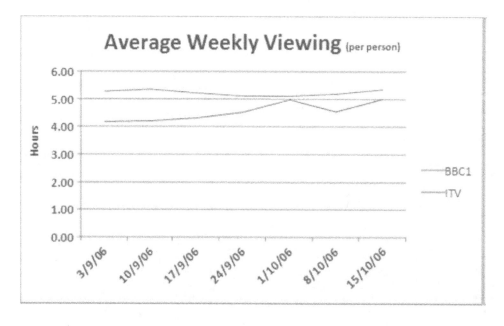

Spruce it up a bit by adding a bit of fill color, rounded edges, and shadow. You've already done this previously, so we won't go through it again. When you're done, it may look like ours:

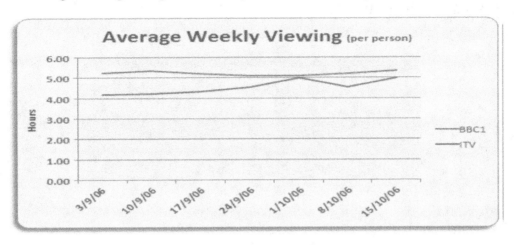

3.13 PREDICTING FUTURE VALUES WITH EXCEL CHARTS

Excel can help you make predictions about future values, or help you spot a linear trend. What we'll do in this section is set up something called a Trendline. We'll use an X, Y Scatter chart for this. We'll look at future income predictions based on what was earned in previous years. If you're a bit confused, don't worry it will all become clear as we go along.

Type the following headings into cells A1 to C1:
Year, Years since 2006, Income
Format the cells if you prefer. Your spreadsheet will then look like this:

	A	B	C
1	Year	Years since 2006	Income
2		.	
3			

Enter the years 2006 to 2019 into cells A2 to A15:

	A	B	C
1	Year	Years since 2006	Income
2	2006		
3	2007		
4	2008		
5	2009		
6	2010		
7	2011		
8	2012		
9	2013		
10	2014		
11	2015		
12	2016		
13	2017		
14	2018		
15	2019		
16			

As an X axis for our chart, we can have the years since 2006. These values will be used in a later formula. In Cells B2 to B15 enter the values 0 to 13:

	A	B	C
1	Year	Years since 2006	Income
2	2006	0	
3	2007	1	
4	2008	2	
5	2009	3	
6	2010	4	
7	2011	5	
8	2012	6	
9	2013	7	
10	2014	8	
11	2015	9	
12	2016	10	
13	2017	11	
14	2018	12	
15	2019	13	
16			

We now need some income values for the years 2006. This is income that has been earned, rather than income that might be earned in the future. We'll then use this hard data to predict future values. Enter some income values, then, into cells C2 to C9. We made up the following values:

	A	B	C
1	Year	Years since 2006	Income
2	2006	0	12300
3	2007	1	15300
4	2008	2	14250
5	2009	3	15900
6	2010	4	16700
7	2011	5	16300
8	2012	6	17100
9	2013	7	16800
10	2014	8	
11	2015	9	
12	2016	10	
13	2017	11	
14	2018	12	
15	2019	13	
16			

We're now ready to insert an X, Y Scatter chart.
Highlight the cells B1 to C9:

	A	B	C
1	Year	Years since 2006	Income
2	2006	0	12300
3	2007	1	15300
4	2008	2	14250
5	2009	3	15900
6	2010	4	16700
7	2011	5	16300
8	2012	6	17100
9	2013	7	16800
10	2014	8	
11	2015	9	
12	2016	10	
13	2017	11	
14	2018	12	
15	2019	13	
16			

This will be the data for our chart.

From the top of Excel, click on the Insert ribbon. From the Charts panel, locate and click on the Scatter charter icon. The icon looks like this:

Select the first item to get a chart with just dots:

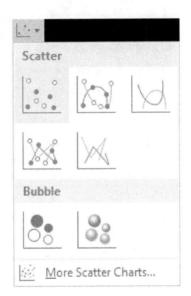

(If you can't see the icon above, click on Recommended Charts. Switch to the All-Charts tab, then select X Y Scatter).

A new chart will then appear on your spreadsheet. It should look like this:

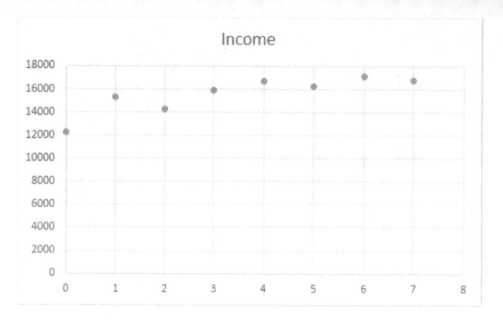

The figures along the bottom, the X Axis, are our years since 2006. The figures on the Y Axis are our income values. The first dot, the one on the far left, tells us that we made just over 12000 at Year 0, (Year 0 is 2006). At Year 1 (2007) we made just under 16000. At Year 2 (2008) we made just over 14000, and so on.

All these dots seem to form a loose line going up from the left. You could add a line yourself using the Shapes item on the Illustrations panel. What you'll then have done is to create a linear regression.

Rather than add the line ourselves, however, Excel can add the line for us. Not only that, but it can also give us the formula it used to create the line. We can use that formula to predict future incomes.

To get the line in Excel select your chart then click on the Add Chart Element tab then click the Trendline option. From the Trendline menu, select Linear Trendline.

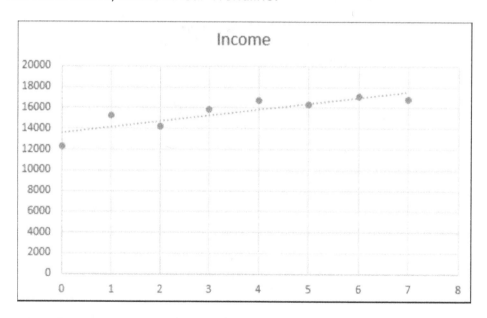

The line represents Excel's best fit for a linear regression. It's trying to put as many as the dots as it can as close to the line as possible.

For Excel users, Click the Layout tab again. Then click the Trendline. From the Trendline menu this time, select More Trendline Options. You'll then see a dialogue box with options the same as the ones in the image below.

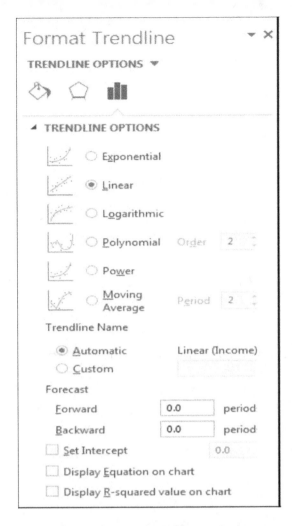

The Trendline option we've chosen is Linear. Have a look at the bottom and check the box next to Display Equation on chart.

When you check the box you should the following equation appear on your chart:

$y = 564.88x + 13604$

This is something called the Slope-Intercept Equation. If you remember you Math lessons from school, the equation is usually written like this (the "b" at the end may be a different letter, depending on where in the world you were taught Math):

$y = mx + b$

In this formula, the letter "m" is the slope (gradient) of the line, and the letter "b" is the first value on the y axis. The x is a value on the X-Axis. Once you have the slope of the line, a value for the X-Axis, and the starting point of the line, you can extend the line, and work out other values on it. This will be the letter "y" in the equation.

Excel has already worked out two values for us, the "m" and the "b". The "m" (the slope) is 564.88 and the "b" is an income value of 13604.

To work out the y values we just need an "x". The "x" for us will be those "Years since 2006" in our B column.

Click inside cell C10 on your spreadsheet, then. Enter the following:

=564.88 * B10 + 13604

Press the enter key and you should find that Excel comes up with a value of 18123.04. This is the predicated income for the year 2014. Use Autofill for the cells B11 to B15. The rest of the predicted values will then be filled in:

	A	B	C
1	Year	Years since 2006	Income
2	2006	0	12300
3	2007	1	15300
4	2008	2	14250
5	2009	3	15900
6	2010	4	16700
7	2011	5	16300
8	2012	6	17100
9	2013	7	16800
10	2014	8	18123.04
11	2015	9	18687.92
12	2016	10	19252.8
13	2017	11	19817.68
14	2018	12	20382.56
15	2019	13	20947.44
16			

So, Excel is predicting we'll earn 18123.04 in 2014. By 2019, it's predicting we'll earn 20947.44.

EXTENDING THE TRENDLINE

In the first part of this tutorial, you saw how to add a Trendline Chart. The type of Trendline we used was a Linear Regression one.
You can get Excel to extend the linear regression line on your chart. Click on your chart to highlight it, bring up the Format Trendline dialogue box again. Expand the Trendline option and select More Options. From the Trendline Options, have a look at the Forecast boxes. Type a 6 into Forward:

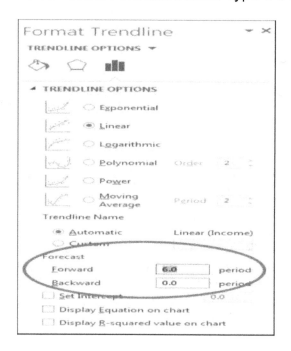

Press the Enter key on your keyboard and you should see the line extend on your chart:

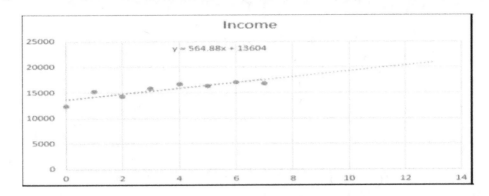

New values have been added to the X-Axis. It now goes from 0 to 14. Trace the vertical line up from 12 until you come to the sloping line. Now trace a straight horizontal line the left, all the way to the Y-Axis, and you can see it reads a value of just above 20000:

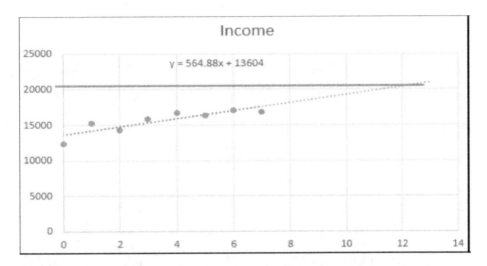

If you look in cell B14 of your spreadsheet, you can see that the value is a more precise 20382.56. So, Excel is predicting we'll earn this much in 2018.
If you want to add the new values as dots to your chart. Click on one of the dots on your chart. This will highlight all the dots:

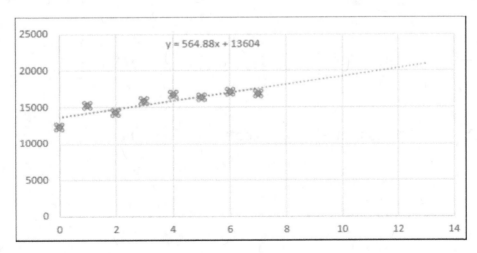

The cells B2 to C9 (the data points) will also be highlighted on your spreadsheet:

	A	B	C
1	Year	Years since 2006	Income
2	2006	0	12300
3	2007	1	15300
4	2008	2	14250
5	2009	3	15900
6	2010	4	16700
7	2011	5	16300
8	2012	6	17100
9	2013	7	16800
10	2014	8	18123.04
11	2015	9	18687.92
12	2016	10	19252.8
13	2017	11	19817.68
14	2018	12	20382.56
15	2019	13	20947.44
16			

To add more data points, drag the blue square in the bottom right of cell C9. Drag it down to cell C15. Now drag the purple square in cell B9. Drag it down to cell B15.

	A	B	C
1	Year	Years since 2006	Income
2	2006	0	12300
3	2007	1	15300
4	2008	2	14250
5	2009	3	15900
6	2010	4	16700
7	2011	5	16300
8	2012	6	17100
9	2013	7	16800
10	2014	8	18123.04
11	2015	9	18687.92
12	2016	10	19252.8
13	2017	11	19817.68
14	2018	12	20382.56
15	2019	13	20947.44
16			

Now have a look at your chart. Click outside of the dots to deselect them:

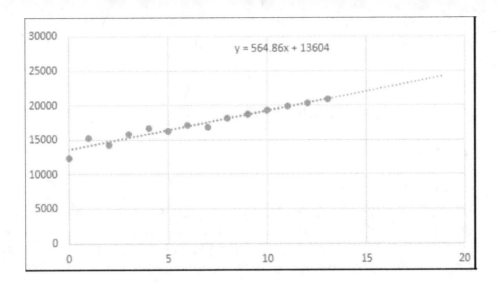

Excel has added the 6 new dots. It has added them all on the line. (They are all on the line because they are predictions, rather than real data.)

And that's it for X Y Scatter charts and linear regression. The above techniques come in quite handy for when you need to show future predictions: predicting revenue streams, predicting future crime statistics, share prices, and lots more besides. If you're looking for work, one thing that may impress an employer is to say that you can do linear progressions on an X Y Scatter chart!

PART FOUR:

FUNCTIONS IN EXCEL

4.1 THE AVERAGE FUNCTION IN EXCEL

If you're trying to work out an average, you're trying to calculate what the most common value is. For example, if a class of eight students took exams, you may want to know what the average exam score was. In other words, what result most students can expect to get. To calculate an average, you'd add up all eight exam scores and divide by how many students took the exam. So, if the total for all eight students was 400, dividing by 8 would get you 50 as the average grade. If any students were below the average, you can tell briefly.

In Excel, there is an easy way to calculate the average of some numbers - just use the inbuilt Average function.

Start a new spreadsheet and enter the following exams scores in cells A1 to A8, as in the image below:

	A	B	C
1	9		
2	7		
3	6		
4	7		
5	8		
6	4		
7	3		
8	9		
9			

Click in cell A9, and we'll see how to use the Average function in Excel. There are two ways we can do this. Try method 1 first.

Method 1
Next to the formula bar, you'll see an FX button. This is the Formula Wizard:

When you click the FX button, you'll see the Insert Function dialogue box appear:

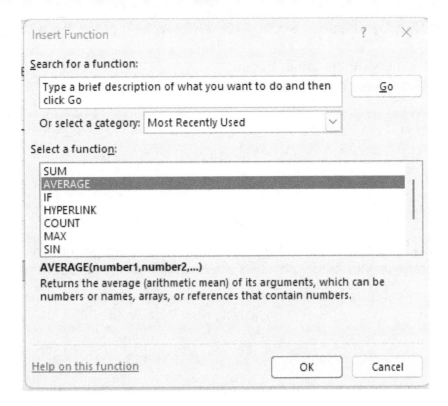

The Insert Function dialogue box shows a list functions. These are the just the common ones. To see more functions, click the drop down list to the right of Select a category. The one we want is displayed under Select a function, though - Average. Click on this, and then click OK.

When you click OK, another dialogue box appears. On this dialogue box, you select the data that you want to include in your function:

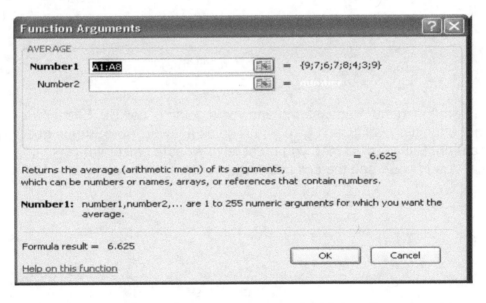

If you look in the Number1 box, you'll see Excel has guessed which cells we want to use for our Average function - A1:A8. It evens gives the answer to the Function - 6.625.

Click OK to insert the function.

Method 2
The second way to enter a Function in Excel is through the panels on the Ribbon. Try this:

- Click inside cell B9 on your spreadsheet. This is where we'll place the Average for the cells A1 to A8.
- Click the Formulas menu at the top of Excel.
- Locate the Function Library panel. Here it is in Excel.

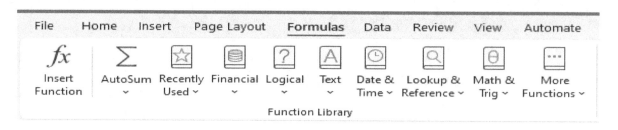

As you can see, in Excel functions are split into categories. The Average function is in a few places. The easiest way to use Average is with AutoSum. Click the down arrow on AutoSum to see the following:

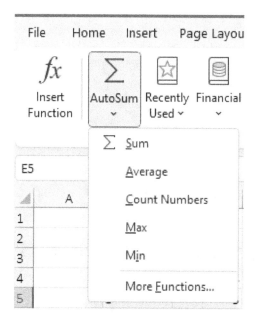

Now click Average from the menu. Because the answer is going in cell B9, Excel doesn't know which cells you want to use in the function, so it can't give you a quick answer. AutoSum is good when the data is in the same row or column. But when it's not, you must tell it what to calculate.

So, click inside cell A1 and you'll see the cell selected.

	A	B	C	D	E
1	9				
2	7				
3	6				
4	7				
5	8				
6	4				
7	3				
8	9				
9		=AVERAGE(A1)			
10		AVERAGE(number1, [number2], ...)			
11					

Hold down your left mouse button over the bottom right blue square, and drag to cell A8:

	A	B	C
1	9		
2	7		
3	6		
4	7		
5	8		
6	4		
7	3		
8	9		
9		=AVERAGE(A1:A8)	
10			

Excel fills in the cells for your function. Let go of the left mouse button, and then press the Enter key on your keyboard. The correct answer is place in cell B9:

B9   ▼   *fx*   =AVERAGE(A1:A8)

	A	B	C	D	E	F
1	9					
2	7					
3	6					
4	7					
5	8					
6	4					
7	3					
8	9					
9		6.625				
10						

You can also find the Average function on the More Functions menu. Click Statistical, and you'll see it there:

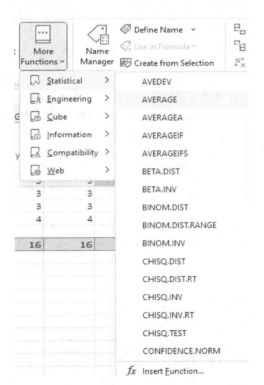

Of course, once you know the correct function, you could simply type it all out in the Formula bar yourself!

Try this exercise.

Exercise
You start your own online business and find that sales for the first week are these:
Monday £120.45
Tuesday £187.43
Wednesday £106.87
Thursday £143.69
Friday £117.52
Saturday £87.93
Sunday £92.12
Use a function to work out how much you earned, on average, each day.

4.2 THE DATE FUNCTION IN EXCEL

There are several different reasons why you would want a Date or Time function in a spreadsheet: If you're running your own company, you might want to record when an order was received and when it was processed. You could then calculate the difference between the two, so that you check how fast the orders were being processed. We'll do that now.

The Excel Date Function

As an example of how to use date functions in Excel, we'll construct as simple spreadsheets for an order form. We'll enter the date an order was taken, the date the order was sent, and how long it took to be processed. So, to make a start, create the spreadsheet below:

	A	B	C	D
1	Date Order Taken	Date Order Sent	Time Taken	
2				
3				
4				
5				

Click inside cell A2, and we'll enter a date. To enter a date, Click on the Formulas menu at the top of Excel. Then locate the Function Library panel. From the Function Library panel, click on Date & Time:

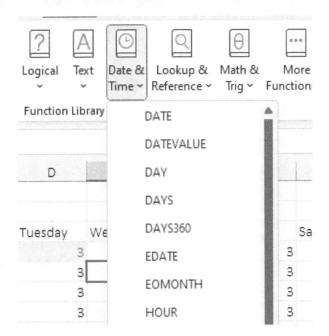

As you can see, there's quite a lot of Date and Time functions! Click on Date from the menu, and you'll get the following dialogue box:

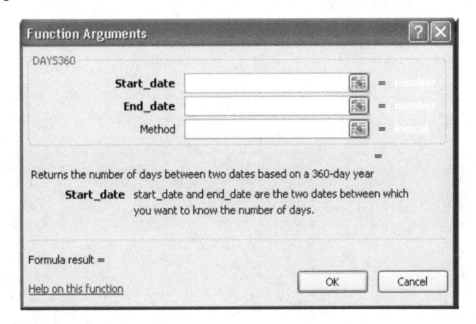

You're now being asked to enter a full date.
- In the Year box, enter 2010.
- In the Month box, enter the number 4.
- In the Day box, enter the number 15.
- Click the OK button.
- Excel will enter the Date in your selected cell, A2 for us.

	A	B	C	D
	A2	▼	f_x =DATE(2010,4,15)	
1	Date Order Taken	Date Order Sent	Time Taken	
2	15/04/2010			
3				
4				

Notice the DATE Function in the Formula bar:
=DATE (2010, 4, 15)

Between the round brackets of DATE, the Year comes first, then the Month, then the Day.
If you want to format your date, as say Monday 15th of April, then you need to click on the Home tab from the Ribbon at the top of Excel. Locate the Number panel, and you'll see Date already displayed:

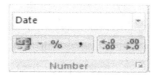

Click the down arrow to see more options:

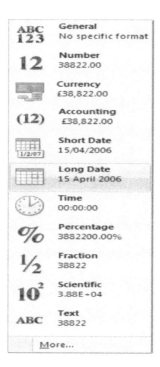

Click the Long Date item. Or click on More at the bottom to see some more Date formats to choose from. Your spreadsheet will then look like this:

	A	B	C	D
1	Date Order Taken	Date Order Sent	Time Taken	
2	15 April 2010			
3				
4				

In cell B2, under your Date Order Sent heading, enter another Date Function. This time, have the date read May 3, 2010:

	A	B	C	D
1	Date Order Taken	Date Order Sent	Time Taken	
2	15 April 2010	03 May 2010		
3				
4				

In cell C2, under Time Taken, we'll work out how many days the order took to be sent out.

The Days 360 Function in Excel

When you want to work out how many days there are between two dates, the function to use is **Days360 ( )**. We want to work out how many days there are between the 15th of April 2010 and the 3rd of May 2010. So, click inside cell C2 and do the following:

Click on the Formulas tab at the top of Excel. Then locate the Function Library panel. From the Function Library panel, click on Date & Time. From the menu, click on Days360 (). You should see the Function Arguments dialogue box appear again. This time, it will look like this:

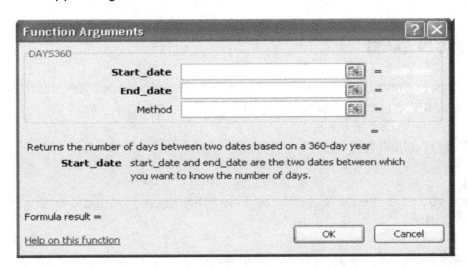

The Days360 function needs a start date and an end date. You can enter your cell references here. So, in the Start date box, enter A2. In the End Date box, enter B2. If you enter the word True in the Method box, Excel will calculate using the European date system. Click OK, to return to your spreadsheet and you might see this:

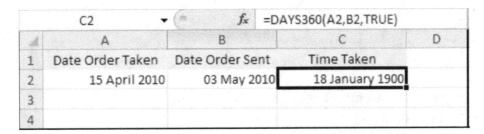

(If your C2 cell has a lot of #### symbols in it, it means that your column is not wide enough. Widen the C column and they'll go away!)

The answer we got was January 18th, 1900! The reason for such a bizarre answer is that we've formatted the C2 cell as a date. But the answer to the Days360 function is not a date - it's a number. If you have the same strange answer, then format your C2 as a number. Your spreadsheet will then look like ours below:

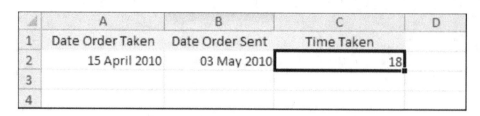

	A	B	C	D
1	Date Order Taken	Date Order Sent	Time Taken	
2	15 April 2010	03 May 2010	18	
3				
4				

So, the difference between the two dates is 18 days.
Entering dates can be straightforward, like cells A2 and B2. But performing calculations with dates can be slightly more complex. To get you some more practice, here's an exercise.

Exercise
Use a Days360 function to work out how many days are left before your next birthday.
Instead of typing out the current date in say cell A2, you can use this inbuilt function:
=Now ()
The Now function doesn't need anything between the round brackets. Once you have today's date, you can enter your birthday in say cell B2.

4.3 TIME FUNCTIONS IN EXCEL

There are several ways to enter the current time in an Excel spreadsheet. Try this:
- Click inside a blank cell on your spreadsheet.
- Click into the Formula Bar at the top.
- Type the following inbuilt function:

= Now ()
Hit the enter key, and you'll get the current date and time. If you only want the time, you can format the cell to get rid of the date part:

- Click on the cell that contains your Now () function.
- From the Excel menu bar, click on Home.
- Locate the Number panel, and you may see Time already set (it might say Custom in later versions of Excel):

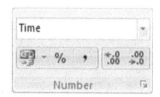

- Click the down arrow to see menu options.
- From the menu, click on Time.
- Click on More to see more Time options.

Excel doesn't update the Time function every second, so it's not like a normal clock. But you can update the Now function to get the correct time. (Well, it's correct if your system clock is correct!)

134

The easiest way to update the Time in Excel is to click inside the cell that holds your Time formula. Then, from the Formulas menu, locate the Calculation panel.

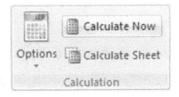

Click the "Calculate Now" button, and Excel will update the time.

Excel also updates the time when you enter another calculation elsewhere in the spreadsheet. For example, click in any other cell on your spreadsheet. Now enter a simple formula like = 2 + 2. When you press the Enter key on your keyboard, Excel will update your time function as well.

To get some practice with using Times in Excel, try the Timetable Project in the next part. You'll also see a different way to enter the time.

A TIMETABLE PROJECT

In this Excel timetable project, we'll set ourselves some chores to do around the house. We'll plan an exact time to start a task, and how long it will take to finish. We'll be adding one time to another.

So, create the same spreadsheet as the one in the image below (you don't need to use the same colors):

	A	B	C	D
1	Job	Start Time	Time Job Takes	
2				
3	Wash Pots			
4	Hoover			
5	Rest			
6	Dust			
7	Windows			
8	Rest			
9				

What we're going to do is enter a Start Time for our chores. This will be 9 in the morning. Then we'll estimate how long it takes to wash the pots, which we'll place in the Time Job Takes column. We'll add the "Time Job Takes" to the "Start Time" to get a new start time for the Hoover chore. But you'll see how it works as we go along.

The first thing to do is to format the Start Time column:

- Highlight the Start Time column, from cell B3 to cell B8.
- From the Excel menu bar, click on Home.
- Locate the Number panel:

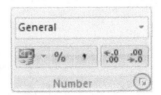

Click on the arrow (circled above) to bring up the Format Cells dialogue box, and then click the Time category:

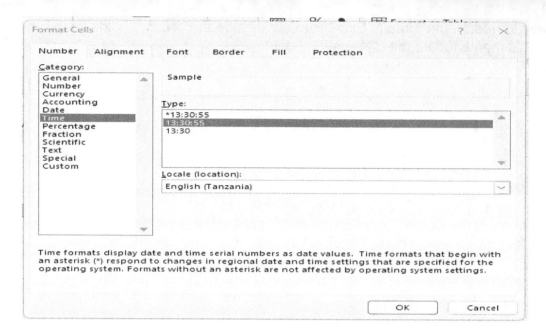

- Under Category on the left, click on Time. Under the time Types on the right, select the first one.
- Don't click OK yet but have a look at the time format that Excel is going to enter.

Excel will enter the hours, then minutes and the seconds. We don't need the seconds. Unfortunately, this version of Excel doesn't give you a time format without seconds. To remedy this, click on Custom under the Category list on the left. Then, under Type, select "h:mm am/pm", as in the image below:

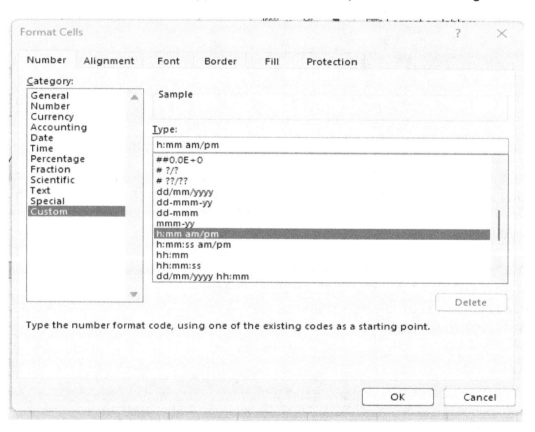

Click OK when you're done.
We'll now enter our first time.

- Click on cell B3, then click inside the formula bar.
- Type in 09:00 (the colon in between the numbers is important)
- Press the enter key on your keyboard.
- Excel will now see cell B3 as a time - 9.00 AM.

	A	B	C	D
1	Job	Start Time	Time Job Takes	
2				
3	Wash Pots	9:00 AM		
4	Hoover			
5	Rest			
6	Dust			
7	Windows			
8	Rest			
9				

There is a simpler way to format a cell as Time, though. Try this:
- Click inside cell C3.
- Click inside the formula bar.
- Type in 0:15.
- Press the Enter key on your keyboard.

Because you included the colon (:), Excel knows that you want to format the cell as a time. The 0:15 then means 15 minutes (We'll assume that we're very fast at washing pots - it's all that practice!).
But your spreadsheet will now look like this:

C3			f_x	00:15:00	

	A	B	C	D
1	Job	Start Time	Time Job Takes	
2				
3	Wash Pots	9:00 AM	00:15	
4	Hoover			
5	Rest			
6	Dust			
7	Windows			
8	Rest			
9				

If we started at 9.00, and the job took 15 minutes, the next start time will be 9.15. We can enter a formula for this:
- Click into cell B4 to highlight it.
- Then click inside the formula bar.
- Enter the following formula:

= B3 + C3
- Press the enter key.
- Excel will place a time of 09:15 AM in cell B4.

| B4 | | fx | =B3 + C3 |

	A	B	C	D
1	Job	Start Time	Time Job Takes	
2				
3	Wash Pots	9:00 AM	00:15	
4	Hoover	9:15 AM		
5	Rest			
6	Dust			
7	Windows			
8	Rest			
9				

The start time for our next chore, then is 9.15 AM. We can use AutoFill for the rest of the B column:
- Click into cell B4 on your spreadsheet.
- Move your mouse the bottom right of cell B4, and the pointer will change shape. When you see the black cross, the AutoFill cursor, hold down your left mouse button and drag down to cell B9.
- Let go of the left mouse button and Excel will AutoFill the other formulas.
- Because we haven't yet entered any other figures for the "Time job Takes" column, a time of 9.15 will appear in all the cells.
- Click onto cell C4 on your spreadsheet.
- Now click into the formula bar at the top, and type in 01:00 (meaning one hour)
- Hit the Enter key on your keyboard and Excel will change all the cells from B5 to B8 to a time of 10:15 AM
- Your spreadsheet should look like ours:

| C4 | | fx | 01:00:00 |

	A	B	C	D
1	Job	Start Time	Time Job Takes	
2				
3	Wash Pots	9:00 AM	00:15	
4	Hoover	9:15 AM	01:00	
5	Rest	10:15 AM		
6	Dust	10:15 AM		
7	Windows	10:15 AM		
8	Rest	10:15 AM		
9				

Complete the rest of the spreadsheet for yourself. Enter these times in the C column:
Rest: 30 minutes
Dust: 30 minutes
Windows: One hour
Rest 30 minutes
If you complete it all correctly, you should have a spreadsheet like ours in the image below:

	A	B	C	D
1	Job	Start Time	Time Job Takes	
2				
3	Wash Pots	9:00 AM	00:15	
4	Hoover	9:15 AM	01:00	
5	Rest	10:15 AM	00:30	
6	Dust	10:45 AM	00:30	
7	Windows	11:15 AM	01:00	
8	Rest	12:15 PM	00:30	
9		12:45 PM		
10				

In the image above, you'll notice that there is a time in cell B9 of 12:45 PM. You should easily be able to get the same figure in your spreadsheet!

Working with date and times can be quite tricky. But it's well worth getting the hang of. We'll move on, though, and have a go at financial functions in Excel.

4.4 FINANCIAL FUNCTIONS

The financial function we're going to explore is called PMT (). You use this function when you want to calculate things like the monthly payment amounts on a loan, or how much per month a mortgage will cost you. We'll use it to work out how much per month a loan will cost us. Here's what we'll do.

We've decided to take out a loan of ten thousand pounds from our friendly banker. We're going to be paying it back over 5 years. The question is, how much per month is this going to cost us?

The PMT () Function in Excel

The PMT () function expects certain values in between its two round brackets. The values that go in round brackets are known as arguments. The arguments for the PMT () function are these:

PMT (rate, nper, pv, fv, type)

Only the first three are needed, and you can miss the final two out if you like.

We'll work out our monthly loan costs with the help of the PMT () function. First, create a new spreadsheet like the one below:

	A	B	C	D	E	F
1	Loan Amount	10000				
2						
3	Interest Rate	Num of Payments	Present Value	Monthly Amount	Total Paid Back	
4						
5						

If you look at cell B1 on the spreadsheet, you'll see a figure of £10, 000. This is the amount we want to borrow. The labels on Row 3 show what else we need: An interest rate, the number of payments we'll make over the 5 years, the present value of the loan, the amount we'll have to pay back each month, and the total amount paid back after 5 years. But we only need the first three for our PMT () function.

In cell A4, we'll need an interest rate. In cell B4 we'll need the number of payments, and in cell D4 we'll need the Present Value of the loan. First is interest rate.

Imagine that the interest rate given to us by the bank is 24 percent per year. For the PMT () function, we need to divide this figure by 12 (the number of months in a year) So try this:
Click into cell A4 on your spreadsheet.
Enter the following formula:
= 24% / 12
Hit the enter key to see the answer appear, as in the image below:

A4			f_x	= 24% / 12	
	A	B	C		D
1	Loan Amount	10000			
2					
3	Interest Rate	Num of Payments	Present Value		Monthly Amount
4	0.02				
5					

Now that we have an interest rate, the next thing we need for the PMT () function is how many payments there are in total. We must pay something back every month for 5 years. Which is a simple formula? So, Click into B4 on your spreadsheet and enter the following:
= 12 * 5
Hit the enter key to see a figure of 60 as the answer.
This figure of 60 is for the second argument of the PMT () function - the nper. This is just the number of payments.
Now that you have a figure in cell A4 (rate), and a figure in cell B4 (nper), there's only one more to go - the Present Value (pv).
The Present Value of a loan, also known as the Principal, is what the loan is worth at the present time. Since we haven't made any payments yet, this is just 10, 000 for us.
Click into cell C4 on your spreadsheet and enter the following:
= B1
Hit the enter key.
You'll see a figure of 10, 000 appear, and your spreadsheet should now look ours below:

	A	B	C	D	E
1	Loan Amount	10000			
2					
3	Interest Rate	Num of Payments	Present Value	Monthly Amount	Total Paid Back
4	0.02	60	10000		
5					
6					

OK, we now have all the parts for our PMT () function: a rate (A4), a nper (B4), and a pv (C4). Try this:
Click into cell D4 on your spreadsheet.
Enter the following function:
= PMT (A4, B4, C4)
Hit the enter key on your keyboard, and you'll see the monthly amount appear. The figure should have been -£287.68. The reason there is a minus sign before the total is because it's a debt: what you owe to the bank.
But this is what your spreadsheet should look like:

	D4		f_x	=PMT(A4, B4, C4)	

	A	B	C	D	E
1	Loan Amount	10000			
2					
3	Interest Rate	Num of Payments	Present Value	Monthly Amount	Total Paid Back
4	0.02	60	10000	-£287.68	
5					
6					

The only thing left to do is see how much this loan will cost us at the end of 5 years. All you need to do here is multiply the monthly amount in cell D4 by the number of payments in cell B4. Enter your formula for this in cell E4, and your spreadsheet will look like ours below:

	A	B	C	D	E
1	Loan Amount	10000			
2					
3	Interest Rate	Num of Payments	Present Value	Monthly Amount	Total Paid Back
4	0.02	60	10000	-£287.68	-£17,260.78
5					

So, a ten thousand pounds loan, at the interest rate the bank is offering, means we'll have to pay back just over 17 thousand pounds over 5 years.

Tweaking the Values

We can change the spreadsheet slightly to give us more control. For your figure in cell B4, the number of payments, you entered 12 * 5. This is 12 months multiplied by 5 years. But what if we wanted to pay the loan back over 10 years, or 15? How much will our monthly payments then be? And will be the final cost of the loan?

Also, the interest rate seems a bit high. What if we can get a better rate elsewhere?

By making a few changes to or spreadsheet, we can amend these values more easily. First, we'll need two new rows.

Inserting New Rows in Excel

We need to insert new rows in our spreadsheet. To insert a new row, click into cell A2. Then click on the Home tab at the top of Excel. Locate the Cells panel, and click the Insert item:

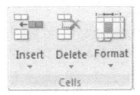

From the Insert menu, click on Insert Sheet Rows:

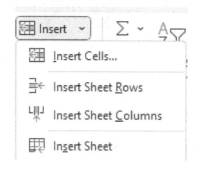

Excel will insert a new row for you. Do this again to get two blank rows. Add two new labels, Num of Years, and Interest. Your spreadsheet sheet will then look like this:

	A	B	C	D	E
1	Loan Amount	10000			
2	Num of Years				
3	Interest				
4					
5	Interest Rate	Num of Payments	Present Value	Monthly Amount	Total Paid Back
6	0.02	60	10000	-£287.68	-£17,260.78
7					

Adapting the PMT Formula

We can adapt the formulas we've entered so far, to make them more usable. As an example, we'll adapt the interest rate.
To get the interest rate for cell A4, we entered a formula:
= 24% / 12
Instead of having the interest rate in cell A4, however, we can place it at the top, in cell B3 on our new Row. We can then alter the interest rate by simply typing a new one in cell B3. To clear all that up, try the following:

- Click inside cell B3, which is the Interest cell in the image above.
- Click inside the formula bar.
- Type in = 24%
- Cell B3 should now read 24.00%

To change the formula for your interest rate, click inside of cell A6. Change the formula from this:
= 24% / 12
to this:
= B3 / 12
Hit the enter key on your keyboard and nothing should change on your spreadsheet. But the difference is that you can enter a new interest rate in cell B3 and see how this effects the loan amounts. Try it out by typing 23% in cell B3:

	B3	▼		fx	=23%	
	A	B	C	D	E	
1	Loan Amount	10000				
2	Num of Years					
3	Interest	23.00%				
4						
5	Interest Rate	Num of Payments	Present Value	Monthly Amount	Total Paid Back	
6	0.019166667	60	10000	-£281.90	-£16,914.28	
7						

As you can see, the interest rate has changed to a rather long figure. But notice the Monthly Amount - it has gone down to £281.90. The total amount we must pay back has changed, too. Play around with the interest rate in cell B3, just to get a feel for how it works.

Exercise

In cell B6 of your spreadsheet, you have the following formula:
= 12 * 5
This calculates the number of months for the loan. Change this formula so that the number of years is coming from B2. Your finished spreadsheet should look like ours below:

	B2	▼		fx	5	
	A	B	C	D	E	
1	Loan Amount	10000				
2	Num of Years	5				
3	Interest	24.00%				
4						
5	Interest Rate	Num of Payments	Present Value	Monthly Amount	Total Paid Back	
6	0.02	60	10000	-£287.68	-£17,260.78	
7						

If you play around with the values in cells B1, B2 and B3 you should be able quickly see the new loan repayments.

4.5 THE IF FUNCTION

The IF function can be quite useful in a spreadsheet. It is used when you want to test for more than one value. For example, has a bill been paid or not? If it has, you can deduct the amount from the money you have left to spend; if it hasn't, keep it on your debt list. Later, you'll see how to use the IF Function to grade student exam scores. If the student has above 80, award an A grade; if the student has below 30, award a failure grade. First, here's what an IF Function looks like:

IF(logical_test, value_if_true, value_if_false,)
The thing to note here is the three items between the round brackets of the word IF. These are the arguments that the IF function needs. Here's what they mean:
logical_test
The first argument is what you want to test for. Is the number in the cell greater than 80, for example?

value_if_true
This is what you want to do if the answer to the first argument is YES. (Award an A grade, for example)

value_if_false

This is what you want to do if the answer to the first argument is NO. (Award a FAIL grade.)
If that's not terribly clear, an example may clear things up. Open a new spreadsheet, and do the following:
- Widen the B column a bit, as we'll be putting a message in cell B1
- Now click in cell A1 and type the number 6.
- Type the following in the formula bar (The right-angle bracket after A1 means "Greater Than".)

=IF (A1 > 5, "Greater than Five", "Less than Five")
Hit the enter key on your keyboard and your spreadsheet should look like ours below:

(Make sure you have all the commas and double quotes in the correct place, otherwise Excel will give you an error message. That right angle bracket (>) is known as a Conditional Operator. You'll meet some others shortly.)
But what we're saying in the IF function is this:
logical_test: Is the value in cell A1 greater than 5?
value_if_true: If the answer is Yes, display the text "Greater than Five."
value_if_false: If the answer is NO, display the text "Less than Five."
So, your first tell Excel what you want to check the cell for, then what you want to do if the answer is YES, and finally what you want to do if the answer is NO. You separate each part with a comma.

Exercise

Try this:
- Click into cell A1.
- Change the 6 into a 4.
- Hit the enter key on your keyboard.
What happens?

Exercise

Now type the number 5 in cell A1. What happens now?
For the last exercise above, Excel should tell you that 5 is "Less than 5"! It does this because the answer to your logical test was NO. We were testing if the number in cell A1 was greater than 5. Since 5 is not greater than 5, the answer to the question is NO. We've told Excel to display a message of "Less than 5", if the answer was NO. In other words, we didn't tell Excel what to do if the value in cell A1 was the same as 5.
The solution to this is to use a different Conditional Operator. We used the Greater Than (>) operator. Here's some more:
< Less Than
>= Greater than Or Equal To
<= Less than Or Equal To
<> Not Equal To
For the second and third operators above, you type an angle bracket followed by the equal's sign. There are no spaces between the two. For the final one, it's a left angle bracket followed by a right-angle bracket.

So, for our exercise, the symbol we should have used was the one for Greater than Or Equal To. Change your IF function to this and try again:
=IF (A1 >= 5, "Greater than or Equal to Five", "Less than Five")

Exercise

Test the A1 cell to see if the value is less than or equal to 5. If it is, display a suitable message. If it's not, display the message "Greater than Five".

4.6 COMPLEX IF FUNCTIONS

The If Functions you've just met are consider simple ones. They can get complex.
Consider our Student Exam problem. The spreadsheet we created to track our students looks like this, from an earlier section:

	A	B	C	D	E	F	G	H	I	J	K
1		Steven	Mary	Ann	Raymond	Mark	Paul	Eliza	Kelly		Averages
2	Maths	76	89	43	48	51	76	87	56		65.75
3	English	55	85	78	61	47	87	91	73		72.13
4	Science	65	82	39	58	52	65	57	45		57.88
5	History	45	91	56	72	49	56	78	56		62.88
6	Geography	51	84	54	64	47	64	67	67		62.25
7	Art	43	63	49	62	39	89	64	63		59.00
8	Computer Studies	63	95	45	59	41	92	89	52		67.00
9	French	35	91	65	26	28	51	92	56		55.50
10											
11	Overall Average	54.13	85.00	53.63	56.25	44.25	72.50	78.13	58.50		

However, we want to display the following grades as well:
A If the student scores 80 or above
B If the student scores 60 to 79
C If the student scores 45 to 59
D If the student scores 30 to 44
FAIL If the student scores below 30.
With such a lot to check for, what will the IF Function look like? Here's one that works:
=IF(B2>=80, "A", IF(B2>=60, "B", IF(B2>=45, "C", IF (B2 >=30, "D", "Fail"))))
Quite long, isn't it? Look at the colors of the round brackets above and see if you can match them up. What we're doing here is adding more IF Functions if the answer to the first question is NO. If it's YES, it will just display an "A".
But look at our Student Exam spreadsheet now:

B14 | f_x =IF(B2>=80, "A", IF(B2>=60, "B", IF(B2>=45, "C", IF(B2 >=30, "D", "Fail")))))

	A	B	C	D	E	F	G	H	I	J	K
1		Steven	Mary	Ann	Raymond	Mark	Paul	Eliza	Kelly		Averages
2	Maths	76	89	43	48	51	76	87	56		65.75
3	English	55	85	78	61	47	87	91	73		72.13
4	Science	65	82	39	58	52	65	57	45		57.88
5	History	45	91	56	72	49	56	78	56		62.88
6	Geography	51	84	54	64	47	64	67	67		62.25
7	Art	43	63	49	62	39	89	64	63		59.00
8	Computer Studies	63	95	45	59	41	92	89	52		67.00
9	French	35	91	65	26	28	51	92	56		55.50
10											
11	Overall Average	54.13	85.00	53.63	56.25	44.25	72.50	78.13	58.50		
12											
13		Steven	Mary	Ann	Raymond	Mark	Paul	Eliza	Kelly		
14	Maths	B	A	D	C	C	B	A	C		
15	English	C	A	B	B	C	A	A	B		
16	Science	B	A	D	C	C	B	C	C		
17	History	C	A	C	B	C	C	B	C		
18	Geography	C	A	C	B	C	B	B	B		
19	Art	D	B	C	B	D	A	B	B		
20	Computer Studies	B	A	C	C	D	A	A	C		
21	French	D	A	B	Fail	Fail	C	A	C		
22											

After the correct answer is displayed in cell B14 on the spreadsheet above, we used AutoFill for the rest!

4.7 CONDITIONAL FORMATTING

You can use something called Conditional Formatting in your Excel spreadsheets. Conditional Formatting allows you to change the appearance of a cell, depending on certain conditions. What we'll do is to color the Overall Averages on our Student Exam spreadsheet, depending on the grade. Here's the spreadsheet we'll be working on.

	A	B	C	D	E	F	G	H	I
1		Steven	Mary	Ann	Raymond	Mark	Paul	Eliza	Kelly
2	Maths	76	89	43	48	51	76	87	56
3	English	55	85	78	61	47	87	91	73
4	Science	65	82	39	58	52	65	57	45
5	History	45	91	56	72	49	56	78	56
6	Geography	51	84	54	64	47	64	67	67
7	Art	43	63	49	62	39	89	64	63
8	Computer Studies	63	95	45	59	41	92	89	52
9	French	35	91	65	26	28	51	92	56
10									
11	Overall Average	54.13	85.00	53.63	56.25	44.25	72.50	78.13	58.50

- Open your Student Exam spreadsheet (You did complete it, didn't you?)
- Highlight the cells with Overall Grades, which should be cells B11 to I11

The Overall Averages range from 44 to 85. We'll color each grade, depending on a scale. A different color will apply to the following grades:

- 50 and below
- 51 to 60
- 61 to 70
- 71 to 80
- 81 and above

So, five different bands, and a color for each. To set the Conditional Formatting in Excel, do the following:

- With your Overall Averages highlighted, click on the Home menu at the top of Excel.
- Locate the Styles panel, and the Conditional Formatting item:

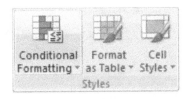

The Conditional Formatting menu gives you various options. The easiest one is the Color Scales option. Select one of these and Excel will color the cell backgrounds for you:

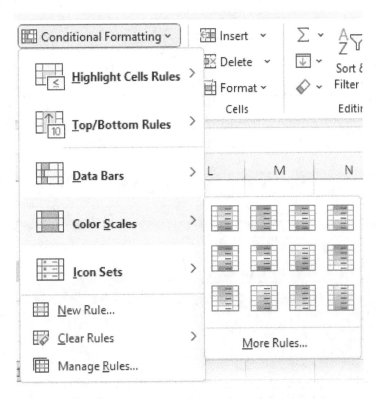

That's not quite what we're looking for, though. We'd like to choose our own values. So, click on More Rules, from the Color Scales submenu. You'll see the following rather complex dialogue box:

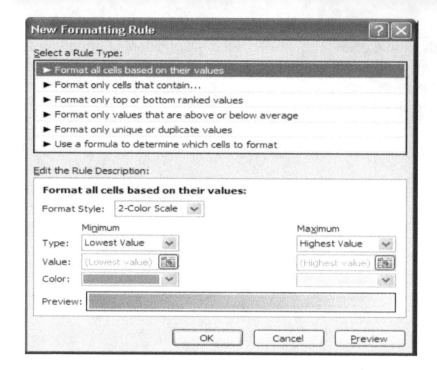

The one we want is the second option, Format only cells that contain. This will allow us to set up our values. When you click this option, the dialogue box changes to this:

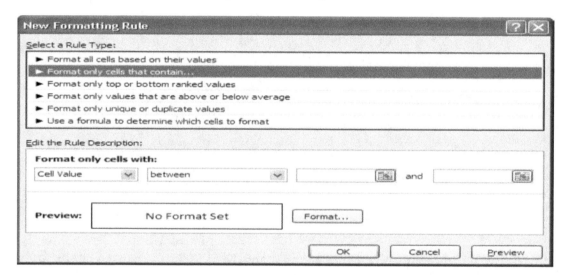

The part we're interested in is the bottom part, under the heading Edit the Rule Description. It says Cell Value and Between, in the drop-down boxes. These are the ones we want. We only need to type a value for the two boxes that are currently blank in the image above. We can then click the Format button to choose a color.

So, type 0 in the first box and 50 in the second one:

Then click the Format button. You'll get another dialogue box popping up. This is just the Format Cells one though. You've met this before. Click on the Fill tab and choose a color. Click OK and you should see something like this under Edit the Rule Description:

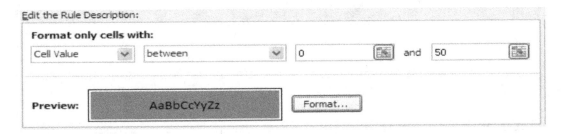

The Preview is showing the color we picked. So, we've said, "If the Cell Value is between 0 and 50 then color the cell Red".
Click OK on this dialogue box to get back to Excel. You should find that one of the cells has turned red. To format the rest of the cells, click on Conditional Formatting on the Styles panel again. From the menu, click on Manage Rules:

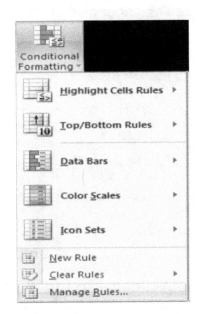

You'll get yet another complex dialogue box popping up! This one:

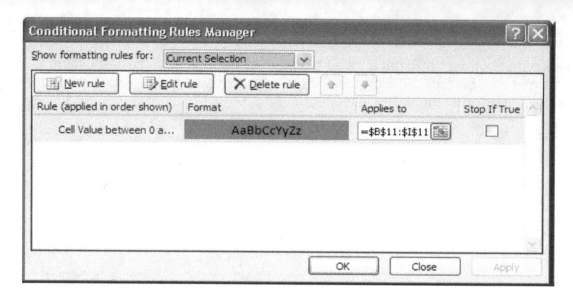

Our first rule is already there - Cell Value Between. The only thing we're doing here is adding New Rules, like the one we've just set up. Click the New Rule button then. You'll see the exact same dialogue boxes you used to set up the first rule. Set a new color for the next scores - 51 to 60. Choose a color and keep clicking OK until you get back to the Rules Manager dialogue box. It should now look something like this one:

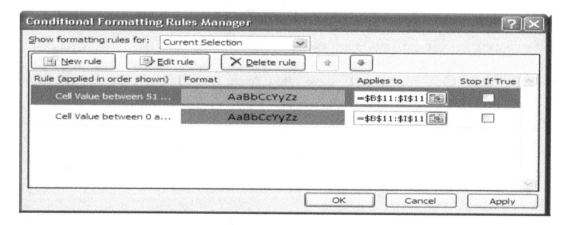

We now must color in our range. Do the rest of the scores, choosing a color for each. The scores are these, remember:

- 50 and below
- 51 to 60
- 61 to 70
- 71 to 80
- 81 and above

When you've done them all, your dialogue box should have five colors:

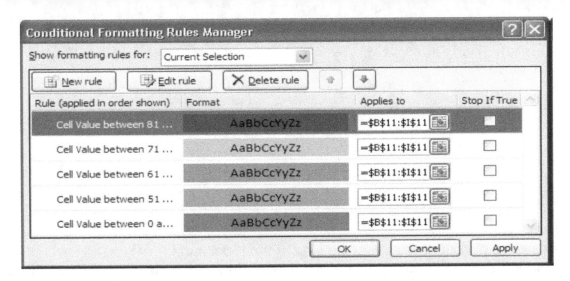

The colors above are entirely arbitrary, and you don't have to select the same ones we did. The point is to have a different color for each range of scores. But click OK when you're done. Your Overall Averages will then look something like this:

	A	B	C	D	E	F	G	H	I
1		Steven	Mary	Ann	Raymond	Mark	Paul	Eliza	Kelly
2	Maths	76	89	43	48	51	76	87	56
3	English	55	85	78	61	47	87	91	73
4	Science	65	82	39	58	52	65	57	45
5	History	45	91	56	72	49	56	78	56
6	Geography	51	84	54	64	47	64	67	67
7	Art	43	63	49	62	39	89	64	63
8	Computer Studies	63	95	45	59	41	92	89	52
9	French	35	91	65	26	28	51	92	56
10									
11	Overall Average	54.13	85.00	53.63	56.25	44.25	72.50	78.13	58.50
12									

Formatting your spreadsheet in this way allows you to see briefly relevant information. In the spreadsheet above, it's obvious who's failing - just look for the red cells!

4.8 COUNTIF IN EXCEL

Another useful function that uses Conditional Logic is CountIF. This one is straightforward. As its name suggests, it counts things! But it counts things IF a condition is met. For example, keep a count of how many students have an A Grade.

To get you started with this function, we'll use our Student Grade spreadsheet and count how many students have a score of 70 or above. First, add the following label to your spreadsheet:

H	I	J	K	L
Eliza	Kelly		Num of Students Above 70	
87	56			
91	73			
57	45			
78	56			
67	67			
64	63			
89	52			
92	56			
78.13	58.5			

As you can see, we've put our new label at the start of the K column.
We can now use the CountIF function to see how many of the students scored 70 or above for a given subject.
The CountIF function looks like this:

COUNTIF (range, criteria)

The function takes two arguments (the words in the round brackets). The first argument is range, and this means the range of cells you want Excel to count. Criteria means, "What do you want Excel to look for when it's counting?".
So, click inside cell K2, and then click inside the formula bar at the top. Enter the following formula:
=Countlf (B2:I2, ">= 70")
The cells B2 to I2 contain the Math scores for all 8 students. It's these scores we want to count.
Press the enter key on your keyboard. Excel should give you an answer of 4:

K2			f_x =COUNTIF(B2:I2, ">= 70")	
	A	J	K	L
1			Num of Students Above 70	
2	Maths		4	
3	English			
4	Science			

(If you're wondering where the columns B to, I have gone in the image above, we've hidden then for convenience's sake!)
To do the rest of the scores, you can use AutoFill. You should then have a K column that looks like this:

	A	J	K	L
1			Num of Students Above 70	
2	Maths		4	
3	English		5	
4	Science		1	
5	History		3	
6	Geography		1	
7	Art		1	
8	Computer Studies		3	
9	French		2	
10				

By using CountIF, we can see briefly which subjects' students are doing well in, and which subjects they are struggling in.

Exercise

Add a new label to the L column. In the cells L2 to L9, work out how many students got below 50 for a given subject. You should get the same results as in the image below:

	A	K	L	M
1		Num of Students Above 70	Num of Students Below 50	
2	Maths	4	2	
3	English	5	1	
4	Science	1	2	
5	History	3	2	
6	Geography	1	1	
7	Art	1	3	
8	Computer Studies	3	2	
9	French	2	3	
10				

4.9 SUMIF

Another useful Excel function is SumIF. This function is like CountIf, except it adds one more argument:

SUMIF (range, criteria, sum_range)

Range and criteria are the same as with CountIF - the range of cells to search, and what you want Excel to look for. The Sum_Range is like range, but it searches a new range of cells. To clarify all that, here's what we'll use SumIF for. (Start a new spreadsheet for this.)

Five people have ordered goods from us. Some have paid us, but some haven't. The five people are Elisa, Kelly, Steven, Euan, and Holly. We'll use SumIF to calculate how much in total has been paid to us, and how much is still owed.

So, in Column A, enter the names:

	A	B	C	D
1	Customer			
2				
3	Elisa			
4	Kelly			
5	Steven			
6	Euan			
7	Holly			
8				

In Column B enter how much each person owes:

	A	B	C	D
1	Customer	Total Goods Ordered		
2				
3	Elisa	£120.00		
4	Kelly	£134.00		
5	Steven	£123.00		
6	Euan	£145.00		
7	Holly	£156.00		
8				

In Column C, enter TRUE or FALSE values. TRUE means they have paid up, and FALSE means they haven't:

	A	B	C	D
1	Customer	Total Goods Ordered	Has Paid	
2				
3	Elisa	£120.00	TRUE	
4	Kelly	£134.00	FALSE	
5	Steven	£123.00	FALSE	
6	Euan	£145.00	TRUE	
7	Holly	£156.00	FALSE	
8				

Add two more labels: Total Paid, and Still Owed. Your spreadsheet should look something like this one:

	A	B	C	D
1	Customer	Total Goods Ordered	Has Paid	
2				
3	Elisa	£120.00	TRUE	
4	Kelly	£134.00	FALSE	
5	Steven	£123.00	FALSE	
6	Euan	£145.00	TRUE	
7	Holly	£156.00	FALSE	
8				
9				
10	Total Paid			
11	Still Owed			
12				

In cells B10 and B11, we'll use a SumIF function to work out how much has been paid in, and how much is still owed. Here's the SumIF function again:

SUMIF (range, criteria, sum_range)

So, the range of cells that we want to check are the True and False values in the C column; the criteria is whether they have paid (True); and the Sum_Range is what we want to add up (in the B column).

In cell B10, then, enter the following formula:

=SUMIF (C3:C7, TRUE, B3:B7)

When you press the enter key, Excel should give you the answer.

	A	B	C	D
	B10	▼	f_x =SUMIF(C3:C7, TRUE, B3:B7)	
	A	B	C	D
1	Customer	Total Goods Ordered	Has Paid	
2				
3	Elisa	£120.00	TRUE	
4	Kelly	£134.00	FALSE	
5	Steven	£123.00	FALSE	
6	Euan	£145.00	TRUE	
7	Holly	£156.00	FALSE	
8				
9				
10	Total Paid	265		
11	Still Owed			
12				

So, 265 is has been paid in. But we told SumIF to first check the values in the cells C3 to C7 (range). Then we said look for a value of TRUE (criteria). Finally, we wanted the values in the B column adding up, if a criterion of TRUE was indeed found (sum_range).

Exercise

Use SumIF to work out how much is still owed. Put your answer in cell B11.

4.10 ADVANCED EXCEL

It is not necessary that you read this section to use Excel.

If you have a good grasp of the issues already described in the book, you can already use Excel with good results.

This section goes a little further and looks at the more advanced types of formulas and functions you can use.

In other words, this section will raise your level from skilled user to advanced user.

Excel has a myriad of functions that you can use in your formulas, and sometimes the biggest challenge seems to be able to find your way around to get what you need.

It is these features that I will describe in this section. You can then explore the more specialized functions on your own.

NESTED FUNCTIONS

When you write a formula, you can use functions as arguments inside other functions.

You might want to calculate the square root of a sum of a series of cells.

It could look like this:

=s qroot(SUM(B2:B20))

Here we have a SUM function as argument in a SQ ROOT function.

It is not that hard, but if you start working with many nested functions in a formula, you need to keep your tongue straight in the mouth in order to place start and end brackets in the right places.

MATHEMATICAL AND STATISTICAL FUNCTIONS

This is an overview of the main mathematical and statistical functions.

Sum

Calculates the sum of numbers in one or more cell regions.

Average

Calculates the average number in one or more cell regions.

Empty cells and cells with text are ignored in the calculation.

SQROOT (Square Root)

This Function is self-explanatory. It calculates the square root of a number.

Trigonometric Functions

Excel has the usual trigonometric functions SIN () COS () TAN () and the inverse arcsin(), arccos() and arctan. In addition, there are the

hyperbolic versions, like SINH (), COSH () and TANH ().

Please note that angles are expressed in radians.

PI

PI () makes no arguments but is just the known constant with 14 decimal places.

ABS (Absolute Value)

Has nothing to do with car brake systems but returns the absolute value of a number.

If the argument is a positive number, only the number is returned.

If the argument is a negative number, the number is returned as a positive number.

SHORTEN

SHORTEN (number, number of decimal places) returns a number with the specified number of decimal places.

It is almost like rounding off but SHORTEN ignores rounded off and simply deletes the excess decimals.

If the argument "Decimal Places" is left out, the number is shortened to 0 decimal places, that is an integer.

ROUND OFF

Works like SHORTEN and uses the same arguments. But here the figure is rounded off normally.

The argument "Decimal places" is not optional in the ROUND OFF function

MIN (Minimum Value)

MIN (value1, value2, ...) or MIN (cellarea1;cell area2; ...) Returns the smallest value of a quantity.

The argument is one or more cell areas and/or two or more values.

MAX (Maximum Value)

Is of course the opposite of the MIN function.

SUMIF (Conditional Sum)

Adds numbers in a table together on condition that they, or other values in same row, meet a certain criterion.

In the following example we have a small table with two columns.

The first column contains some text, and the second some figures.

In the example, we put the figures together that are on the same line as the text "blue":

RAND (Random Numbers)

This function has no arguments but returns a random number between 0 and 1.

The value changes over time when making a new calculation in the spreadsheet.

COUNT (Number of Cells with Numbers)

COUNT (cell area) Counts the number of cells in an area that contains numbers.

Empty cells and cells with text are not counted. Cells with formulas that return figures are counted.

Logical functions

Logical functions do not return a number, but a response in the form of TRUE, FALSE or an error code.

I often use the logical functions to get a formula to choose between different methods depending on some values.

AND Function

AND (statement1 statement; 2; ...) evaluates one or more statements. If all allegations are true, it returns TRUE.

If only one statement is false, it returns FALSE.

An example might be:

=AND (2<3;4=4;5>4) returns TRUE, since all statements are accurate.

=AND (2<3;4=4;5=4) returns FALSE, since one of the statements is wrong.

In practice we often use cell references or nested functions instead of numbers.

OR Function

Is used in the same way as the AND function, but here returns TRUE if just one claim is correct.

NOT Function

NOT (statement) returns FALSE if the allegation is true and TRUE if the allegation is false.

You could also say that it lies about the outcome!

IF FUNCTION

IF (statement; TRUE" range"; FALSE"range") evaluate a statement. If the claim is TRUE, it returns that which is in the true part, otherwise it returns what is in the false part.

IF.ERROR Function

IF. ERROR (formula; result if error) shows the result of a formula if it can be calculated.

If it cannot be calculated, an alternative outcome is shown. It could, for example, be if you try to divide something by 0, which returns an error.

=IF.ERROR(2*3;10) returns 6 since the formula 2*3 can be calculated.

=IF.ERROR(2/0;10) returns 10, since the formula tries to divide 2 by 0, which returns an error value. Instead, it shows the alternative result.

4.11 THE LOOKUP FUNCTION

The LOOKUP function in Excel is used to search one column of data and find data in the corresponding row. For example, if you are searching for a column of employee IDs the LOOKUP function can find, say, employee number 12345 in the ID column. Once it has found the ID 12345 it then can return data from that same row. Let's create a spreadsheet to clear things up.

(The LOOKUP function we'll examine is called a VECTOR LOOKUP. There's also an ARRAY LOOKUP, but we won't cover that here.)

Create the following simple spreadsheet:

	A	B	C	D	E	F
1	Item Number	Shoe Type	Price		LOOKUP Result	
2	312	Stiletto	85			
3	583	Kitten heel	57			
4	229	Stacked heel	70			
5	471	Platforms	30			
6	823	Wedge	35			
7	773	Sandals	37			
8	612	Mules	40			
9	982	Pumps	45			
10	156	Slingbacks	48			
11						

So, we have item numbers in the A column, then a list of products in the B column. Prices are in the C column. Our spreadsheet only has 10 items, but it could have hundreds, even thousands of entries. What we'd like to do is to take an item number and see what Shoe Type, or what Price corresponds to that item number. An item number of 229, for example, would return either "Stacked heel" or a price of 70. We can use the LOOKUP function for this.

The LOOKUP function needs three between its round brackets. It needs these:

LOOKUP (value_to_lookup,data_to_search,results_column)

The value to lookup would be 229 in our example. This is in the A column. So, the data to search is A2 to A10. If we want the results to come from the B column, we need the data from B2 to B10. If we wanted the Price to be returned, the data would be in C2 to C10.

So, we can add the following LOOKUP function to return a Shoe Type:

=LOOKUP (229, A2:A10, B2:B10)

Or this one, for the Price:

=LOOKUP (229, A2:A10, C2:C10)

So, click into cell F1 in your spreadsheet. Click inside the formula bar and enter:

=LOOKUP (229, A2:A10, B2:B10)

When you've entered the formula, press Enter. You'll immediately see that there is a problem:

	F1	▼		fx	=LOOKUP(229, A2:A10, B2:B10)			
	A		B		C	D	E	F
1	Item Number		Shoe Type		Price		LOOKUP Resu ⓘ	#N/A
2	312		Stiletto		85			
3	583		Kitten heel		57			
4	229		Stacked heel		70			
5	471		Platforms		30			
6	823		Wedge		35			
7	773		Sandals		37			
8	612		Mules		40			
9	982		Pumps		45			
10	156		Slingbacks		48			

Cell F1 has #N/A in it, indicating there the value is not available. The reason for this error is that LOOKUP needs the data you're searching to be sorted, otherwise problems like this will occur.

To sort the data, highlight the cells A2 to C10. With the cells highlighted, click the Editing panel on the Home ribbon. From the Editing panel, click Sort & Filter. Then select Smallest to Largest from the menu:

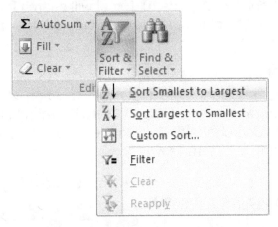

When your data is sorted, LOOKUP should produce the correct result:

	A	B	C	D	E	F
					F1	▾ ⬤	*fx*	=LOOKUP(229, A2:A10, B2:B10)			
1	Item Number	Shoe Type	Price		LOOKUP Result	Stacked heel
2	156	Slingbacks	48			
3	229	Stacked heel	70			
4	312	Stiletto	85			
5	471	Platforms	30			
6	583	Kitten heel	57			
7	612	Mules	40			
8	773	Sandals	37			
9	823	Wedge	35			
10	982	Pumps	45			

So, the Shoe Type for item number 229 is Stacked heel.

There are some things to be aware of with the LOOKUP function. If the item you're searching for is less than the smallest item in your data, then an error will occur. As an example, try entering 100 as the first number in your LOOKUP function:

=LOOKUP (100, A2:A10, B2:B10)

The N/A error should appear in cell F1 again.

If LOOKUP can't find your value, then it will return the highest value lower than your number. So, for us, the highest value lower than 229 is 156.

As well as entering a number like 229 you can change it to a cell reference. So, the formula could be this:

=LOOKUP (F1, A2:A10, B2:B10)

In cell F1 you'd enter the value you want to search for.

The value you're searching for doesn't have to be a number. You can enter text as well. For example, suppose we wanted to return the item number for Mules. We'd do it like this:

=LOOKUP ("Mules", B2:B10, A2:A10)

The value to search for is now text, surrounded by double quotes. For us, the text is in the B column, B2 to B10. The Item Number is in the A column, A2 to A10. Excel will search for the text "Mules" in the B column and return the Item Number from the A column. (Instead of typing Mules in double quotes you can change it to a cell reference, if you prefer.)

4.12 THE VLOOKUP FUNCTION

In the previous section, you learned about the LOOKUP function in Excel. There's another type of LOOKUP function you can use, however, called the VLOOKUP (there's also an HLOOKUP, but we won't cover that). VLOOKUP is used to search the first column of your spreadsheet for a value. If the value is found, you can return data from any cell in that row.

The VLOOKUP function needs three pieces of information, separated by commas. (You can also add an optional fourth value, which we'll see in a moment)

LOOKUP (value_to_lookup, data_to_search, results_column, [match_case])

To illustrate VLOOKUP, create the following spreadsheet (or you can use the same one from the previous section).

	A	B	C	D	E	F
1	Item Number	Shoe Type	Price	Discount	VLOOKUP ITEM NUMBER	583
2	156	Slingbacks	£48.00	5%	VLOOKUP SHOE TYPE	
3	229	Stacked heel	£70.00	15%	VLOOKUP PRICE	
4	312	Stiletto	£85.00	20%	VLOOKUP DISCOUNT PRICE	
5	471	Platforms	£30.00	20%		
6	583	Kitten heel	£57.00	10%		
7	612	Mules	£40.00	15%		
8	773	Sandals	£37.00	5%		
9	823	Wedge	£35.00	5%		
10	982	Pumps	£45.00	5%		
11						

Notice that the data in the first column, Item Number, is sorted lowest to highest. If you don't sort your data, then LOOKUPS can give you problems.

The item number we want to look up is in cell F1 and is a value of 583. We can use VLOOKUP to return the Shoe Type associated with item number 583.

Click inside cell F2 to select it, then click inside the formula bar at the top. Enter the following formula:

=VLOOKUP (F1, A2:C10, 2)

Press the enter key on your keyboard when you have finished typing the formula. You should find a value of "Kitten heel" is returned.

So, the value we want to search for is in F1. The data we want to search is the cells A2 to C10. The column that needs to be returned is column 2. When Excel finds the 583 it sees that this on row 6. The value in Row 6, column 2 is what VLOOKUP returns its answer.

As was mentioned, you can add a fourth argument after the column number. This argument is either TRUE or FALSE and has to do with matching values from what you are searching for (the F1 for us). If you enter a value of TRUE (the default) then Excel looks for an exact match. If no exact match is found, it settles for the next lowest value. As an example, enter 580 in cell F1. When you press enter you should see "Platforms" appear in cell F2. Because we left off a value of TRUE or FALSE as the fourth argument it defaults to TRUE. When Excel can't find a value of 580 it looks at the next value lower than 580, which is 471 for us. This is on Row 5. Row 5, column 2 is "Platforms".

Now click in cell F2 to highlight it. Click inside the formula bar and amend your function to this:

=VLOOKUP (F1, A2:C10, 2, FALSE)

All we've done is added FALSE on the end, but after a comma. Press the enter key on your keyboard and Excel gives you N/A error. It does this because FALSE means "find an exact match". Because we didn't have a value of 580 an error is returned.

Change FALSE to TRUE and try again. You get Platforms as an answer.

Now change the 580 in cell F1 to 150. When you press enter, cell F2 shows the N/A error again. This time, the error occurs because 150 is smaller than the smallest value we have for Item Number.

Change the value in cell F1 to 612. Hit the enter key and you'll find that "Mules" appears in cell F2.

4.13 HOW TO REFERENCE FORMULAS AND DATA ON OTHER WORKSHEETS

You don't have to have all your data on one worksheet. In fact, it's common practice to create lots of worksheets in the same workbook. In this lesson, you'll see how to reference a formula that is on a different worksheet. This comes in handy if, for example, you have 12 worksheets, one for each month of the year. You can then create another worksheet that holds things like totals for the entire year. We'll do that now.

- Open Excel (If it's already open, close the project you're currently working on and open a new blank workbook.)
- Locate Sheet1, Sheet2, and Sheet3 at the bottom of Excel Rename these to May, June, July (Right click, and select Rename from the menu)

Click on the May sheet, and enter the same data as in the following image:

B1		fx	1250
	A	B	C
1	May Sales	£1,250	
2			
3			

Click on the June sheet and enter the following:

H9		fx	
	A	B	C
1	June Sales	£2,472	
2			
3			

Then click on the July sheet and enter the following:

H14		fx	
	A	B	C
1	July Sales	£4,187	
2			
3			

We now need to create a new worksheet. So, click on the New Worksheet icon at the bottom of Excel, the one to the right of July in the image below:

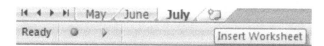

The new worksheet will be called Sheet4 by default. Rename it to Annual Total, and your workbook will look like this at the bottom (If your new worksheet is not at the end, hold down your left mouse button on the worksheets name. Keep it held down and drag to the end):

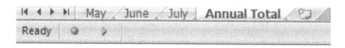

We're now going to add up the figures on the May, June, and July worksheets, and put the answer on the Annual Total worksheet.

Add a label to your Annual Total worksheet:

	A	B	C
1	Yearly Total		
2			
3			

Then click inside cell B1.

To reference data on another worksheet, you use the exclamation mark. This is commonly called a Bang! So, enter this in cell B1 of your Annual Total worksheet:

=May! B1

So, we start with an equal's sign (=), and then type the Name of the worksheet we want to reference (May). After the exclamation mark (bang), we have the cell we want to reference (B1). If you just type B1 by itself, Excel will assume that you meant the current worksheet.

When you press the enter key, you should see this on your Annual Total worksheet:

	A	B	C
1	Yearly Total	£1,250	
2			
3			

This is the same figure as the one on your May worksheet. To add up all our monthly worksheets, just reference them in the same manner:

=May!B1 + June!B1 + July!B1

So, click inside cell B1 of your Annual Total worksheet and replace your formula with the one above. Press the enter key and you should see the answer:

	A	B	C	D
1	Yearly Total	£7,909		
2				
3				

So, when you want to include figures or formula from other worksheets, remember to include the name of the worksheet followed by a bang.

4.14 A BUSINESS INVOICE WITH VLOOKUP

In the last section, you saw how to use VLOOKUP. We're now going to create a business invoice that relies heavily on VLOOKUP. This is intermediate excel, so don't worry too much if you don't understand it all - just skip ahead to the next section and come back to it later.

But the Invoice we're going to create looks like this:

EBAOMS COMPUTER EDUCATION					
Address:	Singida,Mawenzi,Ipuli,223	**Email:**	h@mail,com		
Postcode:	223	**Website:**	df.com		
Invoice number:	1586				
Customer Name:	Salum, Harun	**Phone:**	7890456		
Address:	Singida,Mawenzi,Ipuli,223	**Email:**	h@mail,com		
Date	**Description**	**Quantity**	**Price**	**Total**	
06/07/2023	blue tshirt	6	TSh500	TSh3,000	

The invoice works by typing an invoice number into cell B5 (the 12343 in the image above). When you press the Enter key on your keyboard, data will be pulled from two more worksheets. The two worksheets contain Customer Data and Sales Data. The Customer's Name, Address, etc, gets pulled from a worksheet called Customer_Data, and information about what the customer bought is pulled from a worksheet called Sales_Data. All the information on the Invoice worksheet is automatically updated when you change the invoice number is cell B5.

Let's make a start, then. Create a new spreadsheet for this. Name the first worksheet Customer_Data, and the second one Sales_Data. The third worksheet should be changed to Invoice. Your new spreadsheet will then look like this at the bottom:

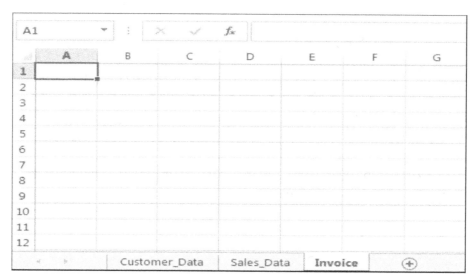

Click on your Customer Data worksheet to select it. On the first row, enter the following headings:

CUSTOMER_NUMBER

FIRST_NAME

SURNAME

ADDRESS1

ADDRESS2

ADDRESS3

POSTCODE

PHONE

EMAIL

You can format this first row if you like. Make the text bold and change the background colour of the cells. Your Customer_Data worksheet will then look something like this:

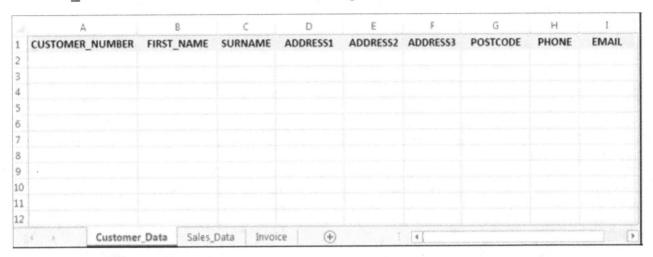

Now enter some data under each heading. Enter data for the customers. Make up the details, just as we have below. The Customer number and the Phone number columns should be formatted as Text. You can leave the other Columns on General. Your worksheet will then look like this:

Now click on your Sales_Data worksheet to select it. On the first row, enter the following headings (make sure you format the columns as below, as well):

INVOICE_NUMBER General

CUSTOMER_NUMBER Text

DATE Date

DESCRIPTION General

QUANTITY General

PRICE Currency

TOTAL Currency

Format the first row however you like. It should then look like this:

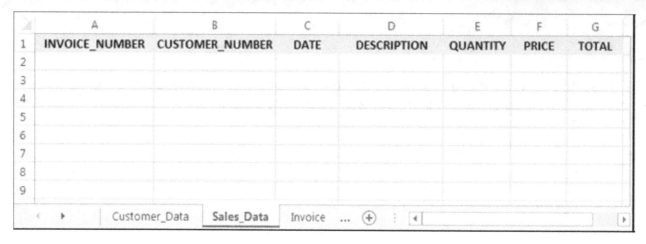

Notice that the first row also has a Customer_Number column. This will contain the same number from the Customer_Data worksheet.

Now enter some data. You can use the same data as ours below, our just make up your own:

INVOICE_NUMBER	CUSTOMER_NUMBER	DATE	DESCRIPTION	QUANTITY	PRICE	TOTAL		
1235	1	04/09/2023	red hat	5	TSh200.00	TSh1,000		
1586	2	06/07/2023	blue tshirt	6	TSh500.00	TSh3,000		
1456	3	07/08/2023	heater	5	TSh800.00	TSh4,000		

The invoice number can be anything you like. But you need to get the Customer Number from your Customer_Data worksheet. The customer numbers we used are these:

1, 2, 3.

This means that customer number 1, who is called Musa, has the invoice number 1235; and customer number 2, Harun, has the invoice number 1586. In other words, the same customer numbers are on both the Customer_Data worksheet and the Sales_Data worksheet.

Now that we have customer and sales data set up, we can turn our attentions to the actual invoice.

4.15 BUSINESS INVOICE, PART TWO

In the previous lesson, you set up an Excel spreadsheet with three worksheets: Customer Data, Sales Data, and Invoice. You have filled out the customer and sales data. It's now time to set up the invoice.

Click on your Invoice worksheet to select it. Create the following labels:

	A	B	C	D	E	F
1						
2	Address:		Email:			
3	Postcode:		Website:			
4						
5	Invoice Number:					
6						
7	Customer Name:		Phone:			
8	Address:		Email:			
9						
10	Date	Description	Quantity	Price	Total	
11						
12						
13				Sales Tax:		
14				Final Total:		
15						

The cell A11, under Date, should be formatted as a date. Description and Quantity can be left on General. Price and Total should be formatted as Currency.

This is a very basic invoice, without any formatting. You can format it later, though, if you like. To start pulling data from the other two worksheets, we'll start with the Date, in cell A11.

So, click inside cell A11. Now enter the following VLOOKUP formula:

=VLOOKUP (B5,Sales_Data!A2:Sales_Data!G5,3)

Just to refresh your memory, inside of the round brackets of the VLOOKUP function, we have three pieces of information:

VLOOKUP (value_to_lookup, data_to_search, results_column)

For us, the value we want to lookup is the invoice number in cell B5. The data to search can be found on the Sales_Data worksheet, in cells A2 to G4. (If you added more rows to your sales data then you need to change the G4 to whatever cell is the end of your data.) The column we want, the Date column, is column 3 (Column C).

After you've entered the formula, press the enter key on your keyboard. You should see #N/A appear. The N/A stands for Not Available. The result is not available because you haven't entered an invoice number yet. Do that now. Look at your Sales_Data worksheet and locate one of your invoice numbers. Return to the Invoice worksheet and enter your invoice number. Press the enter key on your keyboard and you should see a date appear in cell A11:

The VLOOKUP for the other headings (Description, Quantity, Price, and Total) are very similar. The only thing you need to do here is to change the column number for the final position. So, the VLOOKUP function cell B11 would be this:

=VLOOKUP (B5,Sales_Data!A2:Sales_Data!G5,4)

And the VLOOKUP function cell C11 would be this:

=VLOOKUP (B5,Sales_Data!A2:Sales_Data!G5,5)

Cell D11 is this:

=VLOOKUP (B5,Sales_Data!A2:Sales_Data!G5,6)

And cell E11 is this:

=VLOOKUP (B5,Sales_Data!A2:Sales_Data!G5,7)

Enter the VLOOKUP function for yourself in these cells. Your spreadsheet should now look like this:

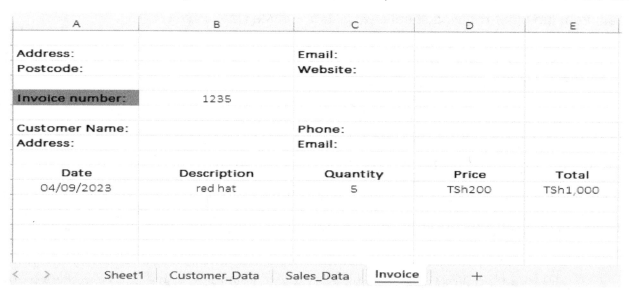

Now change your invoice number in cell B5. When you press the enter key on your keyboard, you should find that your invoice will update all by itself:

	A	B	C	D	E
1					
2	Address:		Email:		
3	Postcode:		Website:		
4					
5	Invoice number:	1586			
6					
7	Customer Name:		Phone:		
8	Address:		Email:		
9					
10	Date	Description	Quantity	Price	Total
11	06/07/2023	blue tshirt	6	TSh500	TSh3,000
12					
13					
14					
15					
16					

Sheet1   Customer_Data   Sales_Data   Invoice   +

We now need to get the customer details for the invoice. This is more complicated. It's more complicated because we need to match a customer number from the Sales_Data worksheet to a customer number from the Customer_Data worksheet.

4.16 A BUSINESS INVOICE, PART THREE

In the previous section, you pulled sales details about an invoice. In this section, you'll see how to get the customer details and add them to your invoice.

The problem we face is that the customer data is on a separate worksheet to the sales data. The sales data worksheet is where we have the invoice number. The question then is how to associate an invoice number with the customer's details. The answer is the Customer Number. We have this on both the Customer_Data and the Sales_Data worksheets. We need to select a customer's details where the Customer Number matches on both worksheets.

As an example, take the invoice number 1586 on the Sales_Data worksheet. In the next column, we have a Customer Number, which is customer 2:

A	B
INVOICE_NUMBER	CUSTOMER_NUMBER
1235	1
1586	2
1456	3

This Customer Number is also on the Customer_Data worksheet:

	A	B	C
	CUSTOMER_NUMBER	FIRST_NAME	SURNAME
	1	Musa	Hakan
	2	Harun	Salum
	3	Lilian	Francis

We can use nested VLOOKUPs to pull data from both worksheets where the customer number matches, and then insert just the customer details into the Invoice worksheet.

Nested VLOOKUPs

You can nest one VLOOKUP function inside of another. The technique can be quite tricky to understand, so you may need to re-read this a couple of times!

Let's do the Phone number and email address first, as we'll use CONCATENATE as well as nested VLOOKUPs in the name and address fields, which will add another layer of complexity.

Click inside of cell D7 of your Invoice worksheet. Now click inside of the formula bar at the top of Excel and enter the following: (You can enter yours on one line. You can just copy and paste the formula below)

=VLOOKUP(VLOOKUP(B5,Sales_Data!A2:Sales_Data!B5,2),Customer_Data!A2:Customer_Data!I5, 8)

Press the enter key on your keyboard and you should see a phone number appear in cell D7. This phone number is coming from the Customer_Data worksheet. But how does it work?

First, have a look at what's needed for a single VLOOKUP again:

VLOOKUP(value_to_lookup, data_to_search, results_column)

The first item between the round brackets is value_to_lookup. Previously, we just entered a cell reference here. This cell reference was B5, which was the invoice number. This time, however, we don't need the invoice number from the Sales_Data worksheet. We need the Customer Number. This is in the cell next to the invoice number. Our inner VLOOKUP is designed to get this Customer Number. Here it is:

VLOOKUP(B5, Sales_Data!A2:Sales_Data!B5, 2)

Again, we used B5 as the value to look up. This is the invoice number. The data to search is in the cells A2 to B5 of the Sales_Data worksheet. The result column is column 2, which is the Customer Number.

When this nested VLOOKUP has returned the Customer Number it is used with the outer VLOOKUP:

=VLOOKUP(RETURNED_CUSTOMER_NUMBER,Customer_Data!A2:Customer_Data!I5, 8)

The RETURNED_CUSTOMER_NUMBER above is the result from the inner VLOOKUP. This is then used to search the Customer_Data in cells A2 to I5 of the Customer_Data worksheet. The results column at the end is column 8, which contains the phone number.

Now click inside of cell D8 of your Invoice worksheet. Enter this nested VLOOKUP:

=VLOOKUP(VLOOKUP(B5,Sales_Data!A2:Sales_Data!B5,2),Customer_Data!A2:Customer_Data!I5, 9)

The only difference here is the column number at the end, column 9. This is where we have stored the email address on the Customer_Data worksheet.

Press the enter key on your keyboard and you should see an email address appear in cell D8.

Now that we have an email address and phone number, we can get the customer's name and address. We could have separate cells here: a cell for the first name, a cell for the surname, a cell for the first line of the address, a cell for the next line of the address, and a separate cell for the zipcode/postcode. What we have done, however, is to have one cell for the customer's full name, and one cell for the customer's address. The customer's full name is in cell B7:

| Customer Name: | Salum, Harun | Phone: | 7890456 |
| Address: | Singida,Mawenzi,Ipuli,223 | Email: | h@mail,com |

And the customer's address is in cell B8:

| Customer Name: | Salum, Harun | Phone: | 7890456 |
| Address: | Singida,Mawenzi,Ipuli,223 | Email: | h@mail,com |

If you have a look at the customer's name, you'll see it's in the format LAST_NAME, FIRST_NAME, with a comma separating the two:

Doe, Jane

To get this, we'll need two nested VLOOKUPs, one for the last name and one for the first name. To join the two together, and add a comma, we can use the inbuilt function CONCATENATE. The CONCATENATE function looks like this:

CONCATENATE (TEXT_ITEM_1, TEXT_ ITEM_2, TEXT_ ITEM_3 ...)

You can have up to 255 Text items. A comma is used to separate each Text item. If you want a comma you need to treat it as a Text item. For example, here's our Doe, Jane text using CONCATENATE:

=CONCATENATE ("Doe", ",", "Jane")

So Text_1 is "Doe", Text_2 is "," and Text_3 is "Jane".

Here's our nested VLOOKUP with CONCATENATE (you can copy and paste this):

=CONCATENATE(VLOOKUP(VLOOKUP(B5,Sales_Data!A2:Sales_Data!B5,2), Customer_Data!A2:Customer_Data!C5,3),",",VLOOKUP(VLOOKUP(B5, Sales_Data!A2:Sales_Data!B5, 2), Customer_Data!A2:Customer_Data!C5, 2))

This is a very long and messy formula. So, let's break it down.

=CONCATENATE(VLOOKUP(VLOOKUP(B5, Sales_Data!A2:Sales_Data!B5, 2), Customer_Data!A2:Customer_Data!C5,3),",",VLOOKUP(VLOOKUP(B5,Sales_Data!A2:Sales_Data!B5, 2), Customer_Data!A2:Customer_Data!C5, 2))

The first VLOOKUP gets the surname from the Customer_Data worksheet. This goes as the first Text Item of CONCATENATE. To put the comma in we have ",". This is the second Text Item of CONCATENATE. The third Text item is the other VLOOKUP. This gets the first name from the Customer_Data worksheet.

So, click inside cell B7 on your Invoice worksheet. Click into the formula bar and enter (or copy and paste) the CONCATENATE code above. When you press the enter key on your keyboard you should have the surname and first name just like ours.

The address uses the same technique, but the CONCATENATE formula is even longer. (It's only longer because we need the address lines and the zipcode/postcode. Here it is to copy and paste into cell B8 on your Invoice worksheet:

```
=CONCATENATE(VLOOKUP(VLOOKUP(B5,Sales_Data!A2:Sales_Data!B5,2),Customer_Data!A2:Customer_Data!I5,4),",",VLOOKUP(VLOOKUP(B5,Sales_Data!A2:Sales_Data!B5,2),Customer_Data!A2:Customer_Data!I5,5),",",VLOOKUP(VLOOKUP(B5,Sales_Data!A2:Sales_Data!B5,2),Customer_Data!A2:Customer_Data!I5,6),",",VLOOKUP(VLOOKUP(B5,Sales_Data!A2:Sales_Data!B5,2),Customer_Data!A2:Customer_Data!I5, 7))
```

It looks insanely complicated, but it's just a longer version of the first CONCATENATE. The only difference is that we have more VLOOKUPs and more commas to insert.

Once you've added the new formula, you should have an address in cell B8 of your worksheet.

And that's it! Try it out. Enter a new invoice number into cell B5, one of your invoice numbers from the Sales_Data worksheet. When you press enter, you should see the invoice automatically update itself.

You can format your invoice however you like. Once formatted, the invoice can be printed out and sent to a customer.

One final word on invoices. If you click File > New you should find that Excel comes with some invoice's templates. Most of these templates use the VLOOKUP techniques you have explored in these lessons. Try them out and you should find that you have a better understanding of how the invoice templates work.

PART FIVE:

PROCESSING DATA IN EXCEL

5.1 DATA TABLES IN EXCEL

In Excel, a Data Table is a way to see different results by altering an input cell in your formula. As an example, we're going to alter the interest rate, and see how much a £10,000 loan would cost each month. The interest rate will be our input cell. By asking Excel to alter this input, we can quickly see the different monthly payments. Want to know how much we'd pay back each month if the interest was 24 percent per year. But other banks may be offering better deals. So we'll ask Excel to calculate how much we'd pay each month if the interest rate was 22 percent a year, 20 percent a year, and 18 percent a year.

The formula we need is the Payment one you met in a previous section - PMT (). Here it is again:

PMT (rate, nper, pv, fv, type)

We only need the first three arguments. So for us, it's just this:

PMT (rate, nper, pv)

Rate means the interest rate. The second argument, nper, is how many months you've got to pay the loan back. The third argument, pv, is how much you want to borrow.

Let's make a start then. On a new spreadsheet, set up the following labels:

	A	B	C	D
1		Payment Terms		
2				
3	Interest Rate			
4	Num of Months			
5	Loan Amount			
6				

So, we'll put our starting interest rate in cell B3 (rate), our loan length in cell B4 (nper), and our loan amount in cell B5 (pv).

Enter the following in cells B3 to B5:

	A	B	C	D
1		Payment Terms		
2				
3	Interest Rate	24.00%		
4	Num of Months	60		
5	Loan Amount	£10,000.00		
6				

So, you need to enter 24.00% in cell B3, 60 in cell B4, and £10,000 in cell B5.

We'll enter our formula now. Click inside cell D2 and enter the following:

=PMT (B3 / 12, B4, -B5)

Cell B3 is the interest rate. But this is for the entire year. In the formula, we're diving whatever is in cell B3 by 12. This will get us a monthly interest rate. B4 in the formula is the number of months, which is 60 for us. B5 has a minus sign before it. It's a minus figure because it's a debt.

When you press the enter key on your keyboard, Excel should give you an answer of £287.68.

Now that we have our function in place, we can create an Excel Data Table. First, though, we need to tell Excel about those other interest rates. It will use these to work out the new monthly payments. Remember, Excel is recalculating the PMT function. So, it needs some new values to calculate with.

So, enter some new values in cells C3, C4, and C5. Enter the same ones as in the image below:

	A	B	C	D
1	Payment Terms			
2				£287.68
3	Interest Rate	24.00%	22.00%	
4	Num of Months	60	20.00%	
5	Loan Amount	£10,000.00	18.00%	
6				

We have put the PMT function in cell D2 for a reason. This is one Row up, and one Column to the right of our first new interest rate of 22%. The new monthly payments are going to go in cells D3 to D5. Excel needs the table setting out this way.

So that Excel can work out the new totals, you must highlight both the new values and the Function you're using.

So, highlight the cells C2 to D5. Your spreadsheet should look like this:

	A	B	C	D
1	Payment Terms			
2				£287.68
3	Interest Rate	24.00%	22.00%	
4	Num of Months	60	20.00%	
5	Loan Amount	£10,000.00	18.00%	
6				

As you can see, the cells C2 to D5 are now highlighted. This includes our new interest rate values in the C column, and our PMT function in cell D2. We can now create an Excel Data Table. This will work out new monthly payments for us. So do this:

- From the Excel menu bar, click on Data.

- Locate the forecast panel.

- Click on the "What if Analysis" item:

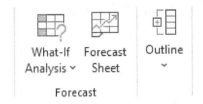

When you click on the "What if Analysis" item, you'll see the following menu:

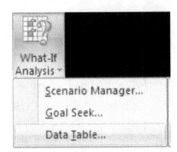

Click on Data Table, and you'll see this small dialogue box:

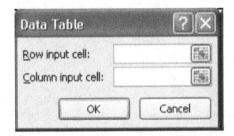

In the dialogue box, there is only a Row input cell or a Column input cell. We want Excel to fill downwards, down a column. So, we need the second text box on the dialogue box "Column input cell". If we were filling across in rows, we would use the "Row input cell" text box.

The Input Cell for us is the one that contains our original interest rate. This is the cell you want Excel to substitute.

So, click inside the Column input cell box and enter B3:

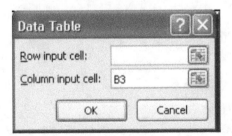

Click OK. When you do, Excel will work out the new monthly payments:

	A	B	C	D
1	Payment Terms			
2				£287.68
3	Interest Rate	24.00%	22.00%	£276.19
4	Num of Months	60	20.00%	£264.94
5	Loan Amount	£10,000.00	18.00%	£253.93
6				

So, if we could get an 18 percent interest rate, our monthly payments would be £253.93.

If you click inside any of the cells D3 to D5, then look at the formula bar, you will see this:

{=TABLE (, B3)}

That's Excel's way of telling you that a Table has been created, based on the input cell B3.

A SECOND DATA TABLE

We'll do one more Data Table, just so that you get the hang of things. This time, we'll use a simpler formula than PMT, and we'll use Rows instead of Columns. This is the scenario:

You have 250 items that you want to sell on eBay. Your unique selling point is this - All items are only £5 each! Except, you feel £5 may be a bit expensive for the goods you're selling! What you want to know is how much profit you'll make if you reduce your prices to £4.50, how much if you reduce to £4.00, and how much for a reduction to £3.50. Assume that everything gets sold.

To start creating your Table, construct a spreadsheet like the one below. Make sure that you start on a new sheet.

	A	B	C	D	E
1	Number of Items	250			
2	Price Per Item	£5.00			
3	Reductions	0	£4.50	£4.00	£3.50
4	Profits				
5					

In cell B1 is the number of items we want to sell (250). Cell B2 has the original price (£5.00). And the Reductions Row has our new values. Cell B3 has a 0 because there's no reduction for £5.00. Row 4 is where our Profits will go.

The formula to work out the profits is simply the Number of Items multiplied by the Price Per Item. So, click inside cell B4 and enter the following formula:

= B1 * B2

Your spreadsheet will then look like this:

	A	B	C	D	E
1	Number of Items	250			
2	Price Per Item	£5.00			
3	Reductions	0	£4.50	£4.00	£3.50
4	Profits	£1,250.00			
5					

So, if we manage to sell all our items at £5, we'll make £1,250. We're a bit dubious, though. Realistically, all our items won't sell at this price! Let's use an Excel Data Table to work out how much profit we'd make at the other prices.

Again, we put the answer in cell B4 for a reason. This is because when you want Excel to calculate a Data Table in Rows, the formula must be inserted one Column to the Left of your first new value, and then one Row down. Our first new value is going in cell C3. So, one column to the left takes us to the B column. One row down is Row 4. So, the formula goes in cell B4.

Next, click inside cell B3 and highlight to cell E4. Your spreadsheet should now look like this one:

	A	B	C	D	E
1	Number of Items	250			
2	Price Per Item	£5.00			
3	Reductions	0	£4.50	£4.00	£3.50
4	Profits	£1,250.00			
5					

Excel is going to use our formula in cell B4. It will then look at the new values on Row 3 (not counting the zero), and then insert the new totals for us. To create a Data Table then, do the following:

- From the Excel menu bar, click on Data.

- Locate the Forecast panel.

- Click on the "What if Analysis" item!

- Select Data Table from the menu.

Just like last time, you'll get the Data Table dialogue box. The one we want now, though, is Row Input Cell. But what is the Input Cell this time?

Ask yourself what you are trying to work out, and what you want Excel to recalculate. You want to work out the new prices. The formula you entered was:

= B1 * B2

Excel is going to be changing this formula. You only need to decide if you want Excel to alter the B1 or the B2. B1 contains the number of items; B2 contains the price of each item. Since we're trying to work out the profits we'd get if we change the price, we need Excel to change B2. So, enter B2 for the Row Input Cell:

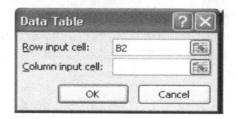

When you click OK, Excel will work out the new profits:

	A	B	C	D	E
1	Number of Items	250			
2	Price Per Item	£5.00			
3	Reductions	0	£4.50	£4.00	£3.50
4	Profits	£1,250.00	£1,125.00	£1,000.00	£875.00
5					

So, setting a price of £3.50 per item, you'd make £875 profit. You'd make £1,000 at £4.00 per item, and £1,125 if you sell for £4.50.

Hopefully, Data Tables weren't too difficult! But they are a useful tool when you want to analyze values that can change.

SCENARIOS IN EXCEL

Scenarios come under the heading of "What-If Analysis" in Excel. They are similar to tables in that you are changing values to get new results. For example, What if I reduce the amount I'm spending on food? How much will I have left then? Scenarios can be saved, so that you can apply them with a quick click of the mouse.

An example of a scenario you might want to create is a family budget. You can then make changes to individual amounts, like food, clothes, or fuel, and see how these changes affect your overall budget.

We'll see how they work now, as we tackle a family budget. So, create the spreadsheet below:

	A	B	C	D	E	F
1		The Family Budget				
2		OUTGOINGS		INCOME		
3	Mortgage	440		1200		
4	Fuel Bills	85				
5	Council Tax	45				
6	Credit Cards	29				
7	Food	280				
8	Clothes	150				
9	Phone Bill	45				
10	Direct Debits	80				
11						
12	Total Outgoings	1154				
13	Income Left			46		
14						

The figure in B12 above is just a SUM function and is your total debts (=SUM (B3:B10). The figure in D3 is how much you must spend each month (not a lot!). The figure in D13 is how much you have left after you deduct all your debts. In cell D13, then, enter =D3 - B12

With only 46 pounds spending money left each month, clearly some changes must be made. We'll create a scenario to see what effect the various budgets cuts have.

- From the top of Excel click the Data menu

- On the Data menu, locate the forecast panel.

- Click on the What if Analysis item, and select Scenario Manager from the menu:

When you click Scenario Manager, you should the following dialogue box:

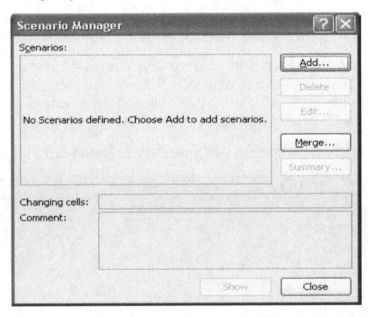

We want to create a new scenario. So, click the Add button. You'll then get another dialogue box popping up:

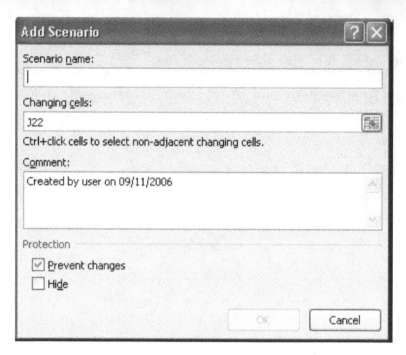

The J22 in the image is just whatever cell you had selected when you brought up the dialogue boxes. We'll change this. First, type a Name for your Scenario in the Scenario Name box. Call it Original Budget.

Excel now needs you to enter which cells in your spreadsheet will be changing. In this first scenario, nothing will be changing (because it's our original). But we still need to specify which cells will be changing. Let's try to reduce the Food bill, the Clothes Bill, and the Phone bill. These are in cells B7 to B9 in our spreadsheet. So, in the Changing Cells box, enter B7:B9

Don't forget to include the colon in the middle! But your Add Scenario box should look like this:

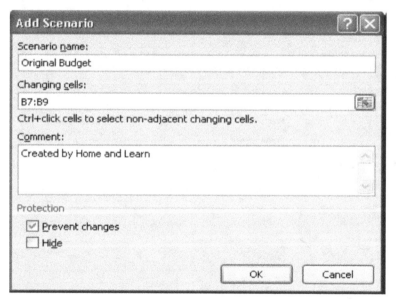

Click OK and Excel will ask you for some values:

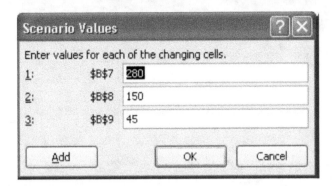

We don't want any values to change in this first scenario, so just click OK. You will be taken back to the Scenario Manager box. It should now look like this:

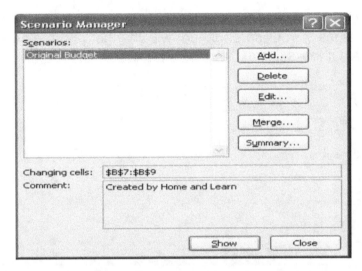

Now that we have one scenario set up, we can add a second one. This is where we'll enter some new values - our savings.

Click the Add button again. You'll get the Add Scenario dialogue box back up. Type a new Name, something like Budget Two. The Changing Cells area should already say B7:B9. So just click OK.

You will be taken to the Scenario Values dialogue box again. This time, we do want to change the values. Enter the same ones as in the image below:

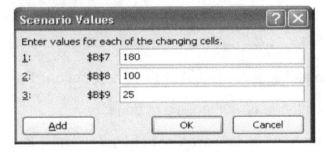

These are the new values for our Budget. Click OK and you'll be taken back to the Scenario Manager. This time, you'll have two scenarios to view:

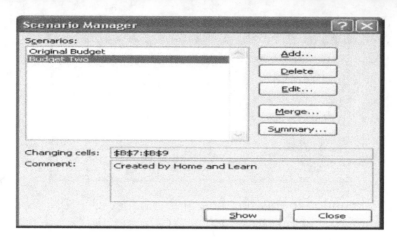

As you can see, we have our Original Budget, and Budget Two. With Budget Two selected, click the Show button at the bottom. The values in your spreadsheet will change, and the new budget will be calculated. The image below shows what it looks like in the spreadsheet:

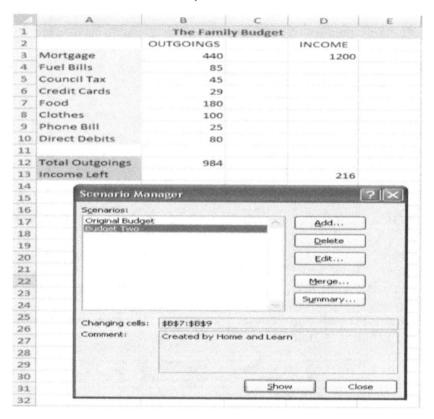

Click on the Original Budget to highlight it. Then click the Show button. The first values will be displayed!

Click the Close button on the dialogue box when you're done.

So, a Scenario offers you different ways to view a set of figures and allows you to switch between them quite easily.

How to Create a Report from a Scenario

Another thing you can do with a scenario is create a report. To create a report from your scenarios, do the following:

- Click on Data from the Excel menu bar.

- Locate the forecast panel.

- On the forecast panel, click What if Analysis.

- From the What if Analysis menu, click Scenario Manager.

- From the Scenario Manager dialogue box, click the Summary button to see the following dialogue box:

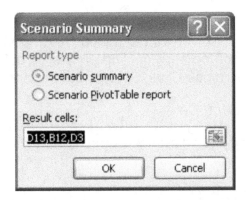

What you're doing here is selecting cells to go in your report. To change the cells, click on your spreadsheet. Click individual cells by holding down the CTRL key on your keyboard and clicking a cell with your left mouse button. Select the cells D3, B12 and D13. If you want to get rid of a highlighted cell, just click inside it again with the CTRL key held down. Click OK when you've selected the cells. Excel will then create your Scenario Summary:

Scenario Summary			
	Current Values:	Original Budget	Budget Two
Changing Cells:			
$B$7	280	280	180
$B$8	150	150	100
$B$9	45	45	25
Result Cells:			
$D$13	46	46	216
$B$12	1154	1154	984
$D$3	1200	1200	1200

Notes: Current Values column represents values of changing cells at time Scenario Summary Report was created. Changing cells for each scenario are highlighted in gray.

All right, it's not terribly easy to read, but it looks pretty enough. Perhaps it will be enough to convince our family to change their ways. Unlikely, but a nice diagram never hurts.

We'll now move on to Goal Seek.

5.2 GOAL SEEK IN EXCEL

Goal Seek is used to get a particular result when you're not too sure of the starting value. For example, if the answer is 56, and the first number is 8, what is the second number? Is it 8 multiplied by 7, or 8 multiplied by 6? You can use Goal Seek to find out. We'll try that example to get you started, and then have a go at a more practical example.

Create the following Excel spreadsheet.

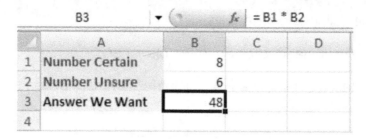

	A	B	C	D
1	Number Certain	8		
2	Number Unsure	6		
3	Answer We Want	48		
4				

In the spreadsheet above, we know that we want to multiply the number in B1 by the number in B2. The number in cell B2 is the one we're not too sure of. The answer is going in cell B3. Our answer is wrong now because we have a Goal of 56. To use Goal, Seek to get the answer, try the following:

- From the Excel menu bar, click on Data.

- Locate the forecast panel and the What if Analysis item. From the What if Analysis menu, select Goal Seek.

- The following dialogue box appears:

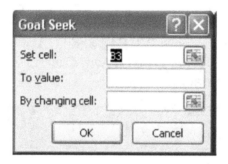

The first thing Excel is looking for is "Set cell". This is not very well named. It means "Which cell contains the Formula that you want Excel to use". For us, this is cell B3. We have the following formula in B3:

= B1 * B2

So, enter B3 into the "Set cell" box if it's not already in there.

The "To value" box means "What answer are you looking for"? For us, this is 56. So just type 56 into the "To value" box

The "By Changing Cell" is the part you're not sure of. Excel will be changing this part. For us, it was cell B2. We weren't sure which number, when multiplied by 8, gave the answer 56. So, type B2 into the box.

You Goal Seek dialogue box should look like ours below.

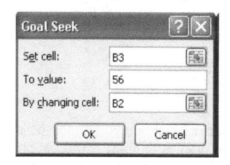

Click OK and Excel will tell you if it has found a solution:

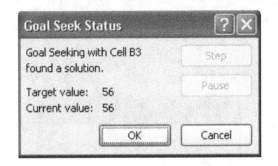

Click OK again because Excel has found the answer. Your new spreadsheet will look like this one:

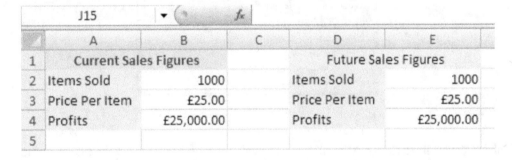

As you can see, Excel has changed cell B2 and replace the 6 with a 7 - the correct answer.

We'll now try a more practical example.

Goal Seek Number Two

Consider this problem:
Your business has a modest profit of 25,000. You've set yourself a new profit Goal of 35,000. Now, you're selling 1000 items at 25 each. Assume that you'll still sell 1000 items. The question is, to hit your new profit of 35,000, by how much do you have to raise your prices?
Create the spreadsheet below, and we'll find a solution with Goal Seek.

	A	B	C	D	E
1	Current Sales Figures			Future Sales Figures	
2	Items Sold	1000		Items Sold	1000
3	Price Per Item	£25.00		Price Per Item	£25.00
4	Profits	£25,000.00		Profits	£25,000.00
5					

The spreadsheet is split into two: Current Sales, and Future Sales. We'll be changing the Future Sales with Goal Seek. But for now, enter the same values for both sections. The formula to enter for B4 is this:

= B2 * B3

And the formula to enter for E4 is this:

= E2 * E3

The current Price Per Item is 25.00. We want to change this with Goal Seek, because our prices will be going up to hit our new profits of 35,000. So, try this:

- From the Excel menu bar, click on Data.

- Locate the forecast panel and the What if Analysis item. From the What if Analysis menu, select Goal Seek.

- The following dialogue box appears:

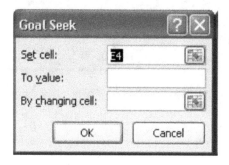

For "Set cell", enter E4. This is where the formula is. The "To Value" is what we want our new profits to be. So, enter 35000. The "By changing cell" is the part we're not sure of. For us, this was the price each item needs to be increased by. This was coming from cell E3 on our spreadsheet. So, enter E3 in the "By changing cell" box. Your Goal Seek dialogue box should now look like this:

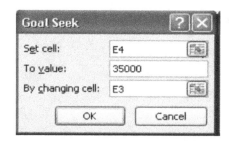

Click OK to see if Excel can find an answer:

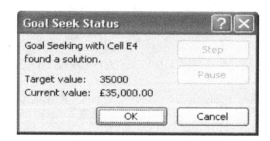

Excel is now telling that it has indeed found a solution. Click OK to see the new version of the spreadsheet:

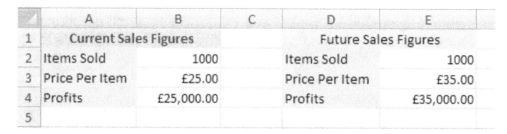

	A	B	C	D	E
1	Current Sales Figures			Future Sales Figures	
2	Items Sold	1000		Items Sold	1000
3	Price Per Item	£25.00		Price Per Item	£35.00
4	Profits	£25,000.00		Profits	£35,000.00
5					

Our new Price Per Item is 35. Excel has also changed the Profits cell to 35 000.

Exercise

You've had a meeting with your staff, and it has been decided that a price change from 25 to 35 is not a good idea. A better idea is to sell more items. You still want a profit of 35 000. Use Goal Seek to find out how many items you'll have to sell to meet your new profit figure.

5.3 ABSOLUTE CELL REFERENCES

An important difference in Excel spreadsheets is between absolute cell references and relative cell references. To see what this is all about, we'll create a simple spreadsheet. This will illustrate relative cell references, which is what we've been using so far.

So, open Excel and enter the same values as in the image below:

In cell B2, you need the following formula:

= A1 + A2

What do you think would happen if we copied and pasted the formula from B2 to cell B3? Let's see:

- Click inside cell B2 to highlight it.

- Click on cell B2 with your right mouse button and select Copy from the menu that appears.

- Now click into cell B3

- Again, right click the cell to get the menu. But this time click Paste.

- Your spreadsheet should now look like ours:

Cell now says 25! We were trying to work out what 20 + 25 was and have the wrong answer. So why did Excel put 25 into cell B3 and not 45?

With cell B3 still highlighted, look at the formula bar at the top of Excel. You should see this formula:

= A2 + A3

Click into B2, however, and the formula is this:

= A1 + A2

The problem is due to cell referencing. When you clicked Copy from the menu, Excel didn't only copy the formula. It looked at where the cells were in the formula, relative to the B2 cell, and copied this as well. From B2, the first cell reference (A1) is up one row, and left 1 column (the red arrow below):

B2   ▾ f_x = A1 + A2

	A	B	C	D	E
1	20				
2	25	45			
3					
4					

The second cell reference (A2) is one column to the left of cell B2:

B2   ▾ f_x = A1 + A2

	A	B	C	D	E
1	20				
2	25	45			
3					
4					

When you clicked into cell B3 and selected Paste from the menu, Excel was not only pasting the formula, but it was also pasting this "up 1, left 1". Look at the two images below. We're now starting at cell B3. Have a look at where the two red arrows are pointing now.

The first cell reference:

	A	B	C
1	20		
2	25	45	
3		25	
4			

The second cell reference:

	A	B	C
1	20		
2	25	45	
3		25	
4			

So, the first red arrow is pointing to cell A2, and the second red arrow is point to cell A3. This is what was copied. Excel then took the formula to mean this:

= A2 + A3

But it should have been this:

= A1 + A2

If you want the correct answer in cell B3, you have to stop Excel from using this Relative Cell Referencing that it's currently doing. What you need is Absolute Cell Referencing.

Absolute cell referencing involves nothing more than placing a dollar symbol ($) before each letter and number.

Click inside of cell B2 on your spreadsheet, and change the formula to this:

= $A$1 + $A$2

Now copy and paste it over to cell B3 again. You should have the correct answer, this time:

	A	B	C	D	E
1	20				
2	25	45			
3		45			
4					

B3 f_x = $A$1 + $A$2

Excel will use Absolute Formula in its own calculation, so it's worth getting used to them. But to recap:

- If you need to copy and paste formulas, use Absolute cell references.

- Absolute referencing means typing a dollar symbol before the numbers and letters of each cell reference (You can mix absolute and relative cell references, though).

5.4 NAMED RANGES IN EXCEL

A Named Range is way to describe your formulas. So, you don't have to have this in a cell:

= SUM (B2:B4)

You can replace the cell references between the round brackets. You replace them with a descriptive name, all your own. So, you could have this, instead:

= SUM (Monthly_Totals)

Behind the Monthly_Totals, though, Excel is hiding the cell references. We'll see how it works, now.

Open Excel and create the spreadsheet below:

The formula is in cell B5, and just adds up the monthly totals in the B column.

Define a Name

Setting up a Named Range is a two-step process. You first Define the Name, and then you Apply it. To Define your name, do this (make sure you have the formula in cell B5):

- Highlight the cells B2 to B4 (NOT B5), then click the Formulas menu.

- Locate the Named Cells panel. Click Define Name

You'll then get the following dialogue box:

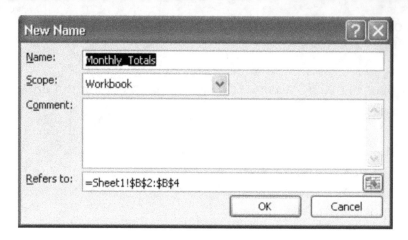

Click OK on the New Name dialogue box. Notice that the Name is our heading of Monthly_Totals.

When you click OK, you'll be returned to your spreadsheet. You won't see anything changed. But what you have done is to Define a Name. You can now Apply it.

Apply a Name

To apply your new Name, click into cell B5 where your formula is, and do this:
- On the Named Cells panel, Click Define Name. From the menu, select Apply Names
- From the Apply Names dialogue box, select the Name you want and click OK:

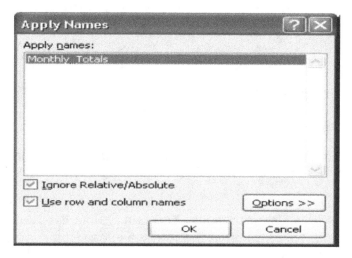

When you click OK, Excel should remove all those cell references between the round brackets, and replace them with the Name you defined:

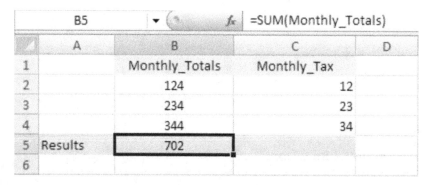

In the image above, cell B5 now says:

=SUM(Monthly_Totals)

The cell references have been hidden. But Excel still knows about them - it's you that can't see them!

Exercise

Study the spreadsheet below, now that we have added another Named Range to cell C5:

	A	B	C	D
	C5		f_x = SUM(Monthly_Tax)	
1		Monthly_Totals	Monthly_Tax	
2		124	12	
3		234	23	
4		344	34	
5	Results	702	69	
6				

Using the same techniques just outlined, create the same Named Range as in our image above. Again, the formula we've used is just a SUM formula:

= SUM (C2:C4)

You need to start with this, before you Define the Name and Apply it.

Using Define Names in Formulas

We'll now use two Named Ranges to deduct the tax from our monthly totals.

So, to define two new Names, do the following:

1. Click inside cell B5 to highlight it

2. From the Formulas menu bar, locate the Named Cells panel, click Define Name > Define Name from the Defined Names panel.

3. From the New Name dialogue box, click into the Name textbox at the top and enter Monthly_Result (with the underscore character)

4. Click OK

5. Click inside cell C5 and do the same as step 2 above. This time, however, enter Tax_Result as the Name

You should now have two new Names defined. We'll now Apply these new names. First, add a new label to your spreadsheet:

	B7	▼	fx	= B5 - C5	
	A	B	C	D	
1		Monthly_Totals	Monthly_Tax		
2		124	12		
3		234	23		
4		344	34		
5	Results	702	69		
6					
7	Final Total	633			
8					

Click into cell B7, next to your new label, and enter the following formula:

= B5 - C5

With the formula in place, we can Apply the two new Names we've just defined:

From the Formulas menu bar, locate the Named Cells panel, click Define Name > Apply Names from the Defined Names panel.

- The Apply Names dialogue box appears.

- Click Monthly_Result to select it.

- Click on Tax_Result to select it:

- Click the OK button.

- Excel will replace your cell references with the two Names you Defined.

- Your spreadsheet should look like ours:

	B7	▼	fx	= Monthly_Result - Tax_Result	

	A	B	C	D
1		Monthly_Totals	Monthly_Tax	
2		124	12	
3		234	23	
4		344	34	
5	Results	702	69	
6				
7	Final Total	633		
8				

If you look at the formula bar, you'll see the two Named Ranges. The formula is easier to read like this. But it's not terribly easy to set up! They can be quite useful, though.

CUSTOM NAMES - CONSTANTS IN EXCEL

You can set up a custom name to be used as a constant. An example of a constant is PI when working with circles. If you need to use PI in formulas you don't need to type out 3.1415 all the time, you can just do this:

= PI()*5

We'll use the spreadsheet below to set up our own custom name:

	A	B	C	D
1	Item Number	Shoe Type	Price	Discount
2	156	Slingbacks	£48.00	
3	229	Stacked heel	£70.00	
4	312	Stiletto	£85.00	
5	471	Platforms	£30.00	
6	583	Kitten heel	£57.00	
7	612	Mules	£40.00	
8	773	Sandals	£37.00	
9	823	Wedge	£35.00	
10	982	Pumps	£45.00	
11				

We'd like to work out a discount, depending on the shoe type. So Slingback shoes might have a discount of 5 percent, but Stacked Heels might have a discount of 12 percent. To set up a custom name, click on the Formulas ribbon at the top of Excel. On the Defined Names panel, select Define Name > Define Name:

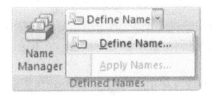

You should see the New Name dialogue box appear:

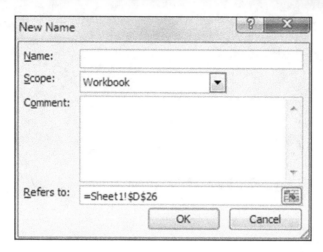

In the Name area at the top, type slingback_discount. In the Refers to textbox at the bottom, you can type a cell reference or a formula. Type =5% in the textbox, though. Then click OK when your dialogue box looks like this:

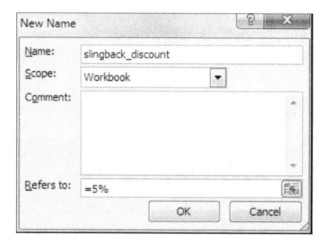

To use your new custom name, click into cell D2 to select it. Then click into the formula bar at the top. Type = C2 *. Then start typing your custom name. As soon as you type the "sl" you'll see a popup box appear:

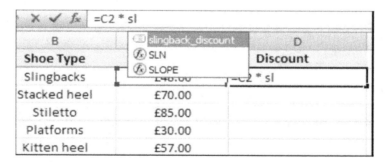

The popup box should have your custom name on the list. Double click it and Excel will add it to your formula. Because we typed =5% in the Refers to textbox of the New Name dialogue box the constant slingback_discount will always be 5%.

Press Enter when the formula is complete, and you should see the discount appear in cell D2:

	D2	f_x	=C2 * slingback_discount	

	A	B	C	D
	Item Number	**Shoe Type**	**Price**	**Discount**
	156	Slingbacks	£48.00	£2.40
	229	Stacked heel	£70.00	
	312	Stiletto	£85.00	
	471	Platforms	£30.00	
	583	Kitten heel	£57.00	
	612	Mules	£40.00	
	773	Sandals	£37.00	
	823	Wedge	£35.00	
	982	Pumps	£45.00	

If you want to delete a custom name, click the Name Manager on the Defined Names panel:

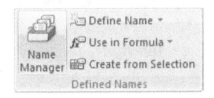

You'll see the following dialogue box appear:

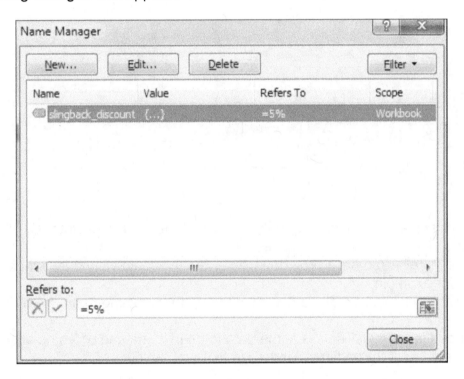

If you want to edit your custom name, click the Edit button at the top. To delete a name, simply select the name from the list then click the Delete button.

5.5 PIVOT TABLES IN EXCEL

A Pivot Table is way to present information in a report format. The idea is that you can click drop down lists and change the data that is being displayed. For example, choose just one student from a drop-down list and view only his or her scores. Pivot tables are a lot easier to grasp when you see them in action. Here's the one we're going to create in this section:

	Student Averages	Subject ▼							
	Month ▼	Art	English	French	History	Maths	Science	Grand Total	
January		89	87	62	81	65	58	74	
March		92	41	56	91	71	41	65	
Febuary		83	51	57	84	72	89	73	
Grand Total		88	60	58	85	69	63	71	

(Row 4: Student — Elisa)

Look at Row 4. This shows that the student is Elisa. If we click Elisa's drop down arrow, we'll see this:

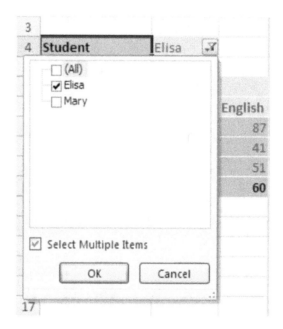

Now we have another student to select (we'll only use two students, for this tutorial). We could untick Lisa, and tick Mary instead. Then her scores would display.

The Subject and Month cells also have drop down lists. So, we could view only January's scores, and just for Art and English, for example.

So, this is a Pivot Table - a report that we can manipulate by selecting items from drop down lists. Let's make a start.

The first thing you need for a Pivot Table is some data to go in it. Instead of typing all the data out, you can copy this data to a new Excel Spreadsheet and save as Pivot table.

Month	Subject	Student	Score
January	English	Elisa	87
January	Maths	Elisa	65
January	art	Elisa	58
January	Art	Elisa	89
January	History	Elisa	81

January	French	Elisa	62
February	English	Elisa	51
February	Maths	Elisa	72
February	Science	Elisa	89
February	Art	Elisa	83
February	History	Elisa	84
February	French	Elisa	57
March	English	Elisa	41
March	Maths	Elisa	71
March	Science	Elisa	41
March	Art	Elisa	92
March	History	Elisa	91
March	French	Elisa	56
January	Engish	Mary	87
January	Maths	Mary	53
January	Science	Mary	35
January	Art	Mary	61
January	History	Mary	58
January	French	Mary	92
February	Engish	Mary	68
February	Maths	Mary	54
February	Science	Mary	56
February	Art	Mary	59
February	History	Mary	61
February	French	Mary	93
March	English	Mary	41
March	Math's	Mary	35
March	Science	Mary	41
March	Art	Mary	48
March	History	Mary	67
March	French	Mary	90

Highlight the data that will be going into your Pivot Table (cells A1 to D37). On the Excel Ribbon, click the Insert tab. From the Insert tab, locate the Tables Panel.

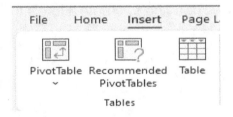

On the Tables panel click Pivot Tables then select from table or range. The Create Pivot Tables dialogue box appears:

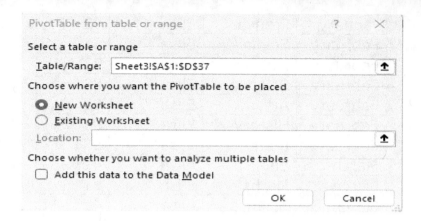

In the dialogue box above, the data that we highlighted is in the Table/Range textbox. You can select different cells by clicking the icon to the right of the Table/Range textbox. You can also specify an external data source, such as a text file, for the data in your Pivot Table.

We've selected a New Worksheet as the place where the Pivot Table will be placed. Click OK.

When you click OK, Excel presents you with a rather complex layout. The area on the right should look something like one of these below, depending on which version of Excel you have:

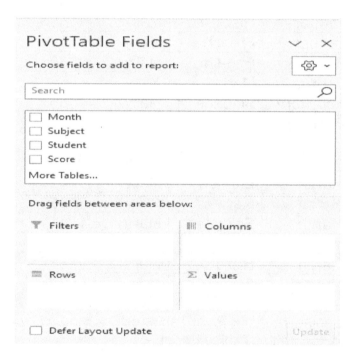

It helps to have a look again at what we're trying to create. Here's the completed Pivot Table again.

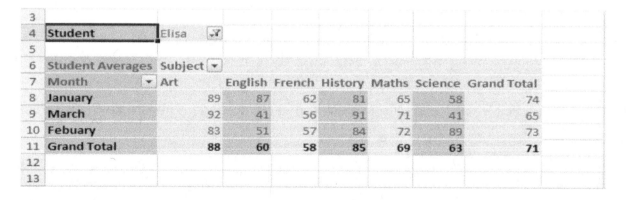

	Student	Elisa						
	Student Averages	Subject						
	Month	Art	English	French	History	Maths	Science	Grand Total
8	January	89	87	62	81	65	58	74
9	March	92	41	56	91	71	41	65
10	Febuary	83	51	57	84	72	89	73
11	Grand Total	88	60	58	85	69	63	71

Now look at the Pivot Table Field List image again, the one above the completed pivot table. It has tick boxes for Month, Subject, Student, and Score. These are column headings from the original spreadsheet data. We've put the Month in cell A7 on our Pivot Table, Subject is in cell B6, Student is in cell B4, and Score is the Average scores in cells C8 to G10. You'll see how it works, though.

The idea is that you tick a box in the Pivot Table Field List, and then drag it to the four areas below. Excel will take care of the rest.

So, tick all four boxes in the field list:

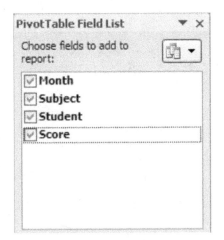

Excel will create a basic (and messy) Pivot Table for you. But we're going to put our 4 fields into the 4 areas below. Here are the 4 areas we can drag to:

For the Report Filter, we want the name of a Student. For the Column Labels, we want the Subject, and for the Row Labels, we'll just have the Month. The Values will be the Average scores.

If you look at the Field areas after you have ticked all four boxes, however, you may see something like this:

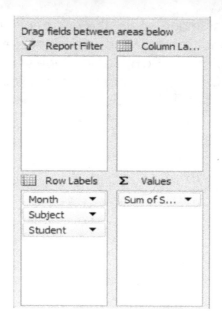

Month, Subject and Student have all been grouped under Row Labels. You can drag and drop these, though.

So, click on Student in the Row Labels box. Hold down your left mouse button, and then drag it in to the Report Filter box. If you don't fancy dragging and dropping, simply click the Student item with your left button. From the menu that appears, select Move to Report Filter

Your Field areas will then look like this:

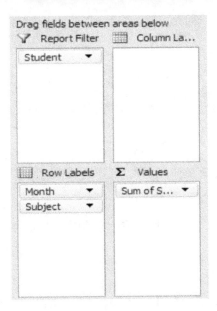

Move Subject from Row Labels to the Column Labels area:

Your Field areas will then look like this:

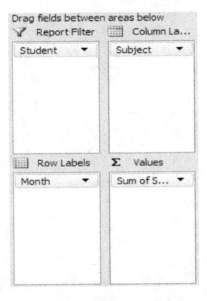

The Pivot Table on your spreadsheet will look a lot different, too. It should be looking like this:

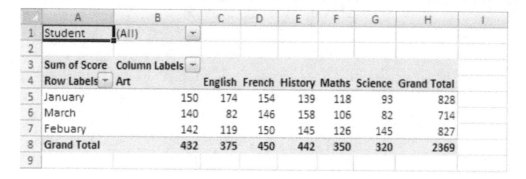

	A	B	C	D	E	F	G	H	I
1	Student	(All)							
2									
3	Sum of Score	Column Labels							
4	Row Labels	Art	English	French	History	Maths	Science	Grand Total	
5	January	150	174	154	139	118	93	828	
6	March	140	82	146	158	106	82	714	
7	Febuary	142	119	150	145	126	145	827	
8	Grand Total	432	375	450	442	350	320	2369	
9									

Our Pivot Table is coming along, but the scores are all wrong, and it needs tidying up a bit.

5.6 PIVOT TABLES - PART TWO

The reason why the scores from our Pivot Table are so strange is because Excel is using the wrong formula. It's using a Sum total when we want it to use an Average.
Here's the Pivot Table so far:

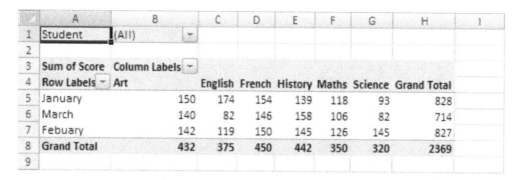

	A	B	C	D	E	F	G	H	I
1	Student	(All)							
2									
3	Sum of Score	Column Labels							
4	Row Labels	Art	English	French	History	Maths	Science	Grand Total	
5	January	150	174	154	139	118	93	828	
6	March	140	82	146	158	106	82	714	
7	Febuary	142	119	150	145	126	145	827	
8	Grand Total	432	375	450	442	350	320	2369	
9									

The numbers have all been added up. But we want averages, instead. To change the formula, click on Sum of Score under the Values field area:

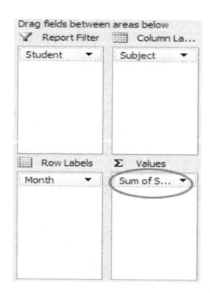

You'll see the following menu:

Select, Field Settings You'll then see the following dialogue box:

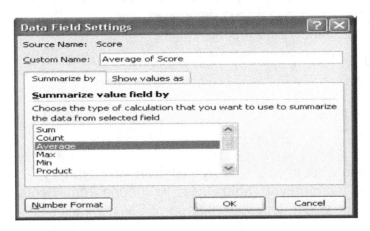

Change the Formula from Sum to Average, and then click OK. Your Average formula won't be formatted to any decimal places. So, highlight your data. On the Home tab in Excel, locate the Number panel. Format your Averages so that it has no decimal places. Your Pivot Table will then look like this:

	A	B	C	D	E	F	G	H	I
1	Student	(All)							
2									
3	Average of Score	Column Labels							
4	Row Labels	Art	English	French	History	Maths	Science	Grand Total	
5	January		75	87	77	70	59	47	69
6	March		70	41	73	79	53	41	60
7	Febuary		71	60	75	73	63	73	69
8	Grand Total		72	63	75	74	58	53	66
9									
10									

Almost there!

Look at cells A3, B3 and A4 above. These all have the not very descriptive names of Average of Score, Column Labels, and Row Labels. You can click inside of these cells and type your own headings, in the same way as you would to enter text in a normal cell.

In the new version of the Pivot Table below, we have renamed these cells. We've also centered the data.

	A	B	C	D	E	F	G	H
1	Student	(All)						
2								
3	Student Averages	Subject						
4	Month	Art	English	French	History	Maths	Science	Grand Total
5	January	75	87	77	70	59	47	69
6	March	70	41	73	79	53	41	60
7	Febuary	71	60	75	73	63	73	69
8	Grand Total	72	63	75	74	58	53	66
9								

Only one thing left to do - spruce up the table by adding a bit of color.

Click anywhere on your Pivot Table to highlight it. Now look at the Ribbon at the top of Excel. You'll notice a Design menu. Click on this to see the various design options.

The Pivot Table Style Options panel is interesting.

Select Banded Rows and see what happens. Now click Banded Columns.

Next to this panel, there are lots of Pivot Table Styles to choose from. Select one that catches your eye. Here's our finished Pivot Table again, only with a different Style:

	A	B	C	D	E	F	G	H	I
1	Student	(All)							
2									
3	Student Averages	Subject							
4	Month	Art	English	French	History	Maths	Science	Grand Total	
5	January	75	87	77	70	59	47	69	
6	March	70	41	73	79	53	41	60	
7	Febuary	71	60	75	73	63	73	69	
8	Grand Total	72	63	75	74	58	53	66	
9									

And here's the original:

	A	B	C	D	E	F	G	H
3								
4	Student	Elisa						
5								
6	Student Averages	Subject						
7	Month	Art	English	French	History	Maths	Science	Grand Total
8	January		89	87	62	81	65	58	74
9	March		92	41	56	91	71	41	65
10	Febuary		83	51	57	84	72	89	73
11	Grand Total		88	60	58	85	69	63	71
12								
13								

There's a lot more you can do with Pivot Tables, but we hope that this introduction has whetted your appetite! But click the dropdown boxes on your Pivot table and play around with them. Change the values you see on the various lists for Student, Subject, and Month.

5.8 FILTERING

Once you have created a table, you must use filters on it.
You use filters to select and show certain data in the table, according to criteria which you have defined.
Excel operates with two different types of filters called "AutoFilter" and "Advanced Filter". AutoFilter is readily available in the column headings when you have defined a table.
Advanced Filter requires a little more work, but it also gives you more options.
In practice AutoFilter is by far the easiest to use, and it can deal with most tasks. Advanced Filter is preferable if you want to filter your table based on values in cells outside of the table you are filtering.

AutoFilter

The AutoFilter is located at the top of the table in the headers.

s ▼	Monda ▼	Tuesda ▼	Wednes ▼	Thursda ▼	Friday ▼	Saturda ▼	Sunday ▼
1	english	a	h	h	j	g	h
2	swahili	a	j	j	k	b	j
3	french	a	l	g	h	p	k
4	turkish	b	k	u	o	o	kb
5	spanish	d	b	j	j	u	jk

As you may have noticed, a button has appeared next to each heading. By clicking the buttons, you will have access to AutoFilter.
In our exercise, we want the table to show French language. The approach is that we look at which columns contain data that we want to find.
Then we take one column at a time and define the criteria for it.
1.Click on the arrow to the right of the header" Monday".
A menu will appear, where you have different options relating to sorting and filtering the column, Do not choose any of the sorting options yet; we will look at that later.

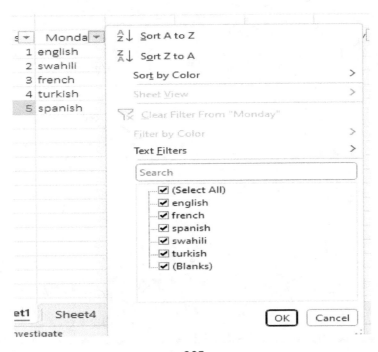

In the menu that appeared you can also see a list of all the values you have typed into the "Monday" column.

In our case it is" French"" English" and" Spanish". Now there's a" tick" next to all three values, which means we have not filtered anything out yet.

2. Click on the selection by Select All to make the markers disappear.

3. Then insert a marker by English. Now it should only be "English".

4. Click on OK.

You have created the first filter, so you are shown only English names.

Notice the spreadsheet row numbers on the left side.

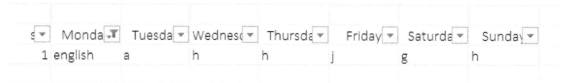

Rows 4, 5,6 and 7 are not displayed, and the rows that contain filtered data are shown in blue row numbers. When row numbers are blue, it means that a filter is active.

It also means that you must think carefully if you want to create two tables with different filters side by side.

Excel hides the entire row in the worksheet when a cell value does not satisfy a given criterion.

So, if you have a second table standing next to the table you are filtering, you may inadvertently hide data in it.

The aim of our exercise was to find English names, so we need to filter by number.

To filter by number before 3, we must define a "custom filter".

5. Click on the small arrow next to the header "s/n."

6. In the menu that appears, point to Number Filters.

7. A submenu will appear. Click on Less Than to open a dialog box.

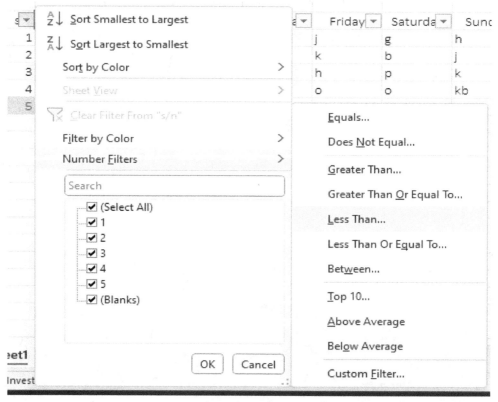

In the dialog box you must indicate that you want to see the rows of the table where the number is "less than" 3.
The dialog box allows you to specify two different criteria, but in this exercise, we only use one.

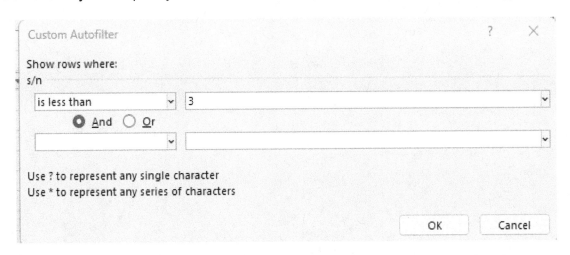

8. Fill out the dialog box as shown in Figure above and click OK
Now we have used filters on the columns," Monday" and" s/n", and the result should look like figure below.

s/n	Monday	Tuesday	Wednesday	Thursday	Friday	Saturday	Sunday
1 english	a	h	h	j	g	h
2 swahili	a	j	j	k	b	j

After all the hard work creating the filters, we must remove them again. Fortunately, it is easy, and it can be done in two ways.
The first method is to remove the filters individually from each column. We will try with" s/n".
9. Click on the filter button next to the header" s/n".
10. In the menu that appears, click on Clear Filter From" s/n."

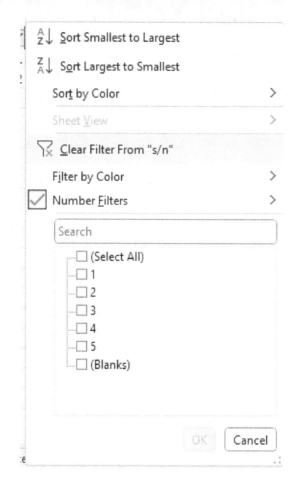

Now the English names in our collection are shown again. The other way of removing filters is used to remove all filters at once.

11. Make one of the cells in the table the active cell.
12. In the Ribbon, click the Data Tab.
13. Click the Filter button on the Sort and Filter tab.

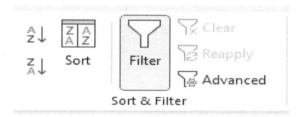

The filters have been removed and all the rows in the table are shown again.

5.9 ADVANCED FILTER

The Advanced Filter works in a completely different way than the AutoFilter. In the Advanced Filter you must create an additional table named "criteria range" with the same column headings as the table that you want to filter.

In the extra table you must specify the criteria and tell Excel where to find the criteria.

Finally, you must also indicate whether you want the table filtered by hiding rows, or by writing the results elsewhere in the spreadsheet.

The latter option means you do not have any hidden rows.

In this exercise, we continue working with the list of our language collection. Again, it seems extremely foolish to filter a table with five rows, but it is easier to understand the different concepts when we are only

First, we must make some space above the table for our Criteria Range.

At least three blank rows above the table are required for the criteria range, since there are some rules that must be observed to make it work:

- The Criteria Range should have column headings, and it must be the same as the column headings in the table to be filtered.
- The Criteria Range should have room for at least one row of criteria.
- There must be at least one empty row acting as the space between the criteria range and the table to be filtered.

In this exercise, there should be room for three series of criteria, so we must have five blank rows above the table to make room for it all.

We can either do this by simply moving the table four rows down, or by inserting four empty rows above it. We choose the latter.

1. Click with the right mouse button on the column heading for row "1". A menu will pop up.
2. Click on Insert (Not to be confused with Paste,).

You have now added an empty row at the top.

We need three more, but since I was born lazy and want to teach you some small tweaks, we will not repeat the same procedure again.

3. Hold the CTRL key on the keyboard down and press the Y key three times. When you hold down the CTRL key and press the Y key, you use the command" Repeat last action". It works for many commands, and in all MS-Office programs. It also works in many other programs.

Now your spreadsheet looks like this:

s/n	Monday	Tuesday	Wednesday	Thursday	Friday	Saturday	Sunday
1	english	a	h	h	j	g	h
2	swahili	a	j	j	k	b	j
3	french	a	l	g	h	p	k
4	turkish	b	k	u	o	o	kb
5	spanish	d	b	j	j	u	jk

Now we need some column headings for the criteria range, Since they are the same as in the table, we can just copy those.

4. Select cell region B6:I6.
5. Hold the CTRL key on the keyboard down and press the C key.
6. Activate cell B1.
7. Hold the CTRL key on the keyboard down and press the V key.

Your spreadsheet should now look like Figure below:

B	C	D	E	F	G	H	I
s/n	Monday	Tuesday	Wednesday	Thursday	Friday	Saturday	Sunday
s/n	Monday	Tuesday	Wednesday	Thursday	Friday	Saturday	Sunday
1	english	a	h	h	j	g	h
2	swahili	a	j	j	k	b	j
3	french	a	l	g	h	p	k
4	turkish	b	k	u	o	o	kb
5	spanish	d	b	j	j	u	jk

Now we can define some criteria, but I would like to try to explain how the criteria range works, because it is not always easy to grasp.

As mentioned, the criteria range is designed as a table with rows and columns.

The columns have headings that correspond to those in the table that is to be filtered according to the criteria. There is obviously a reason why you can write multiple rows of criteria, namely that you can put "AND" or "OR" between the criteria.

Criteria with" AND" in between are placed in the same row Criteria with" OR" between are placed in separate rows.

An example in our table could be that we want to display rows in the table containing names that are English AND prior to 3.

7. Type the word" English" in cell C2.
8. Type" <3" in cell B2 (means" less than 3").
9. Activate another cell in the table you want to filter, for example B6.
10. Choose the Data Tab in the Ribbon.
11. Click on the Advanced button in the Ribbon.

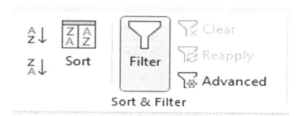

This opens the Advanced filter dialog box, where you must define what is to be filtered and where the criteria are.
12. Make sure that Filter List Locally is selected.
This means that the filter, like AutoFilter is hiding the rows that do not meet the criteria.
13. The field List Range has probably been inserted automatically. It should say" $B$6: $I$11", which is the cell region we are going to filter.
14. In the field Criteria Range you must delete what you have previously inserted, since it is often wrong. With the mouse, mark cell region B1:I2. It should now say "'SHEET 1'! $B$1: $I$2" in this field.
Do not get confused when it says" "Sheet1"!" in front of the cell reference. That is because it is possible to work in multiple sheet tabs in Excel, although we do not for this exercise.
15. Click OK.

B	C	D	E	F	G	H	I
s/n	Monday	Tuesday	Wednesday	Thursday	Friday	Saturday	Sunday
<3	english						
s/n	Monday	Tuesday	Wednesday	Thursday	Friday	Saturday	Sunday
1	english	a	h	h	j	g	h

5.10 ADVANCED FILTER WITH FORMULAS

When using the advanced filter, you are not limited to manually having to write the criteria every time.
You can also write equations where the outcome serves as a criterion in the filter.
For example, if you had to extract values from a table with a filter which is based on a calculation either directly in the filter or because of a complicated calculation elsewhere in the spreadsheet or workbook.
In our previous exercise, you might wish to change to a s/n in cell B9, which you import to cell B2 using the formula" =B9".
If you run the filter, the name with the number 1 will be the only one that meets the criterion.
But what if you want to view the list of all names from before the number 3?
This requires that it says "<3" in the criterion, but how is that done with a formula?
The answer is that you must use what is called a "text string". As you may be aware, Excel knows the difference between numbers and text.
If you want a formula to display text, the text must be surrounded by double quotes.
In our formula, we need to show text in the form of "<" and a number based on the content in cell B9.
This is done by typing = "<" & B9 in cell B2.
In principle the formula should show only two different values, and when you must do something like that you always have to separate the different values with an & symbol.

B	C	D	E	F	G	H	I
s/n	Monday	Tuesday	Wednesday	Thursday	Friday	Saturday	Sunday
<3	english						
s/n	Monday	Tuesday	Wednesday	Thursday	Friday	Saturday	Sunday
1	english	a	h	h	j	g	h

Again, notice the Formula Bar.
When you write a formula where you use the & symbol to display multiple values in succession, Excel will always consider the result as a piece of text.
One would expect that to cause problems when we want to filter according to numbers, but in this case, Excel is clever enough to figure out what you mean.

PART SIX:

MACROS – AUTOMATION

6.1 MACROS – AUTOMATION

Sometimes you repeat the same actions over and over again in a spreadsheet. You may, for example, have an established procedure for formatting cells.

In many cases you can use the automatic formatting of tables, but

often you will just highlight some cells using the grid lines and a frame. This means that you must select the cells, add grid lines, insert a frame and maybe a background color.

After some time, when you have formatted many tables in this way, you may want to look for a way to save some time.

Then "macros" is the answer. A macro is a "tape recording" of a series of actions that you are doing and that you later can play again.

A macro can record virtually everything you do. If you should later feel confident enough to start learning Visual Basic programming language, you will even be able to customize the macros, or turn them into small programs that can do a lot of things.

We will not get that far in this book, but we will attempt to record and play a macro.

RECORDING A MACRO

1. Start by creating a spreadsheet like the one in Figure below.

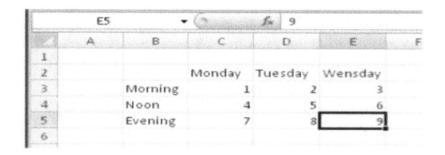

2. Highlight the entire table i.e., cell range B2: E5.
3. In the Ribbon, select the View Tab and click on the Macros
Button located to the far right in the Ribbon.
4. Click on the menu item Record Macro.

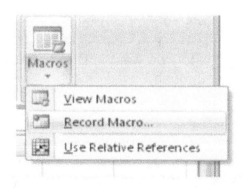

Now opens the window "Record Macro", where you have various choices.

You can write a descriptive name for the macro, and you can assign a hotkey, so you have quick access to the macro.

You must also decide where to save the macro. If you choose This Workbook, it will be available only as long as you are working in the current workbook. If you instead choose Personal Macro Workbook, the macro will always be available.

The "Personal Macro Workbook" is a hidden workbook that is always open when you are working in Excel. Therefore, all macros stored in it will always be available.

5. Give the macro the name" Format_Table". You cannot use spaces in Macro names, so a "_" sign is used instead.

6. Write a "t" as a shortcut. This enables you to activate the macro by holding down the CTRL key on your keyboard and press the T key.

7. Choose to save the macro in Personal Macro Workbook.

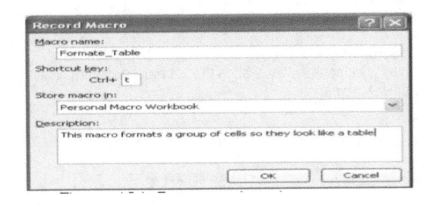

8. You can write a short descriptive text about the macro if you want.

9. Click OK.

Everything you do after this will be recorded in the macro. It is therefore a good idea to plan what the macro should do BEFORE you start recording.

In this case, I have planned everything in advance.

For example, I have already made a cell inside the table the active cell.

Otherwise, I would have to do it now by selecting, for example, cell E5, which would be recorded in the macro. That would not be a good idea, since the macro then always would start by making cell E5 the active cell.

It would make the macro less useful as cell E5 is not always a part of my tables.

10. Right-click inside the table and choose Format Cells from the menu that appears.

11. In the window that opens, click on the Border Tab.

12. Choose the thickest line style and choose a blue colour.

13. Then click on Contour.

14. Choose one of the thin line styles and choose a green colour.

15. Then click on Interior.

16. Click OK.

Now you have formatted the table and the recording must be stopped.

At the bottom left of the screen (next to the text "Ready") there is a small square. It is a "stop button" which stops the macro recording.

17. Click on the Stop button

Now the macro is having completed recording.
There is nothing further to do before we play it.

PLAY A MACRO

18. Select a random cell region.
You decide where and how large the region should be.

19. Hold the CTRL key down on the keyboard and press the T key.
Now the macro is being played, and the cell region you selected gets green grid lines with a blue border around it.
You can record as many macros as you like.
You can view a list of them by clicking the View Tab in the Ribbon, and then click the Macros button. In the menu that appears, click View Macros.

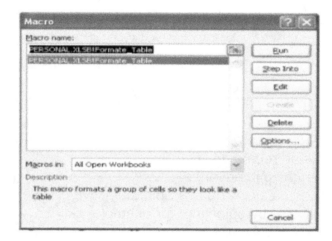

In the macro window, you can play and delete macros. If you know how to program in Visual Basic, you can also edit your macros.
Finally, you can also change the settings to for example assign a different shortcut.

A BUTTON FOR YOUR MACRO

Keyboard shortcuts are good, but you can also add a button into the toolbar, "Quick Access", which activates the macro.

20. Right-click anywhere on the toolbar "Quick Access". It could for example be the disk icon.
21. Click on customize Quick Access Toolbar.
22. In the window that opens, choose the item Customize in the right side.
23. Under "Choose commands from", click Macros.

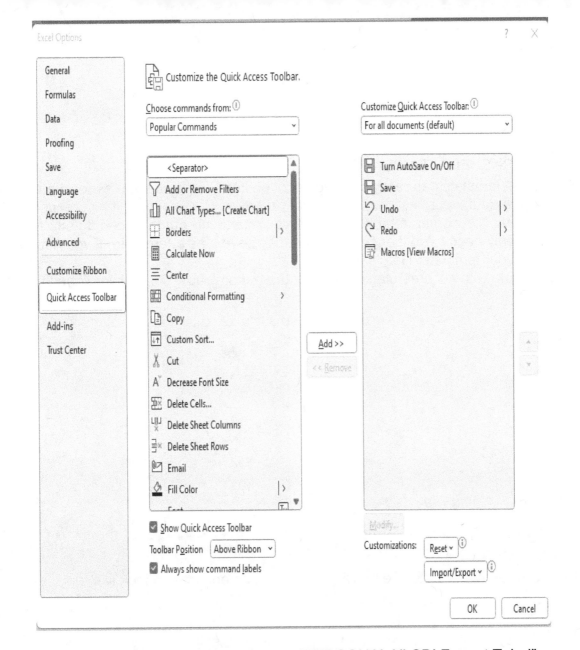

24. In the list, you can now select your macro, called "PERSONAL.XLSB! Format Tabel".
Click it, then click on the Add>> button.
25. Click OK.
Now you have an extra button in the Toolbar" Quick Access". You can go ahead and try it.

PART SEVEN:

ADVANCED EXCEL

7.1 CREATE A WORKSHEET TEMPLATE

Creating a worksheet template can really save you a lot of time. Templates are especially useful if you find yourself having to create the same spreadsheet over and over. For example, if a spreadsheet has sheets for each month of year it becomes a bit if a chore if you must type out the heading and formula for each sheet. Instead, you only need to do it once. Then you can save it as a template. If you need a new month, you can then Insert your template. Here's how.

Open a new workbook, with all three blank sheets at the bottom. Now delete two of the three sheets:

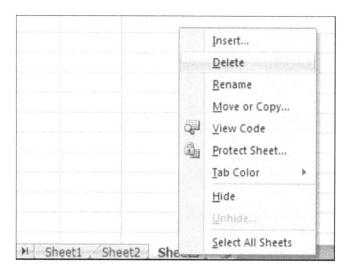

When you have deleted two sheets, the bottom left of your screen should look like this:

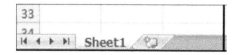

Now create the spreadsheet you want to use as a template. In the image below, we've just set up a simple spreadsheet with Week headings at the top and some labels down the left:

	A	B	C	D	E	F	G
		Week One	Week Two	Week Three	Week Four		Item Totals
1							
2	Food						0
3	Transport						0
4	Bills						0
5	Clothes						0
6							
7	Weekly Totals	0	0	0	0		
8							
9							

G2 f_x =SUM(B2:E2)

Notice how none of the data is filled in for the weeks. The reason there are zeros for the Weekly Totals and the Item Totals is because we have the formulas in place but no data for the weeks. Once it is saved as a template and inserted into a new workbook, then the data can be added. We won't have to add the formulas because they are already in place.

Once you have your spreadsheet looking the way you want it, click the Office button then Save, then under Save As, select Computer. Under the Computer heading, click the Browse icon.

When the Save As dialogue box appears change the Save as type area at the bottom to Excel template. Type a name for your template:

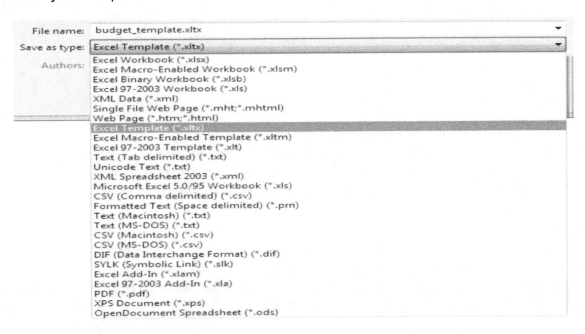

Before clicking Save, notice the file name now ends in xltx, and that it is being saved to a Templates folder inside Excel.

Click the Save button to save your template.

To use your template, close the current worksheet. Create a new blank workbook. Right click a sheet name at the bottom and select Insert from the menu that appears:

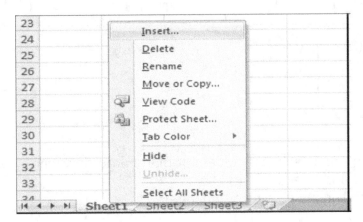

The Insert dialogue box should appear. Your template should be on the list, in the General section:

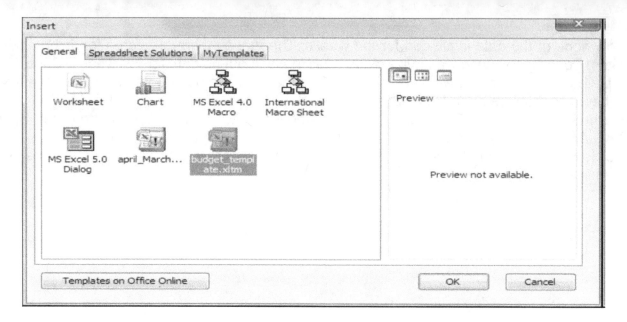

Select your template and click OK. Your template spreadsheet should then be inserted into your new workbook. You can delete any sheets you don't need and rename the template. If you need a new sheet based on your template, right- click a sheet and select Insert from the menu again.

7.2 DROPDOWN LISTS IN EXCEL

If you must type the same data into cells all the time, then adding a drop-down list to your spreadsheet could be the answer. In Excel, this comes under the heading of Data Validation.

In the example below, we have a class of students on a drop-down list. We only must click a cell in the A column to see this same list of students. You'll see how to do that now. Here's a picture of your finished spreadsheet:

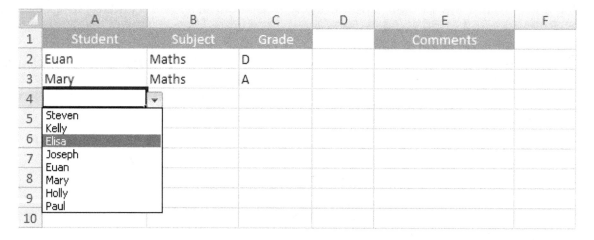

In the image above, we can simply select a student from the drop-down list - no more typing! We can also do the same for the Subject and Grade.

So, create the following headings in a new spreadsheet:

Cell A1 Student

Cell B1 Subject

Cell C1 Grade

Cell E1 Comments

We now need some data to go in our lists. So, type the same data as in the image below. It doesn't need to go in the same columns as ours. But don't type in Columns A, B, C or E:

	E	F	G	H	I
	Comments				
		Steven	Maths	A	
		Kelly	English	B	
		Elisa	History	C	
		Joseph	Geography	D	
		Euan	Art	E	
		Mary	Science	F	
		Holly	Computers		
		Paul	French		

The data in Columns F, G and H above will be going into our list.
Now click on Column A to highlight that entire column:

A1	▼	f_x	Student	
	A	B	C	D
1	Student	Subject	Grade	
2				
3				
4				
5				
6				
7				
8				

With Column A highlighted, click on Data from the Excel Ribbon at the top. From the Data tab, locate the Data Tools panel. On the Data Tools panel, click on the Data Validation item. Select Data Validation from the menu:

When you click Data Validation, you'll see the following dialogue box appear:

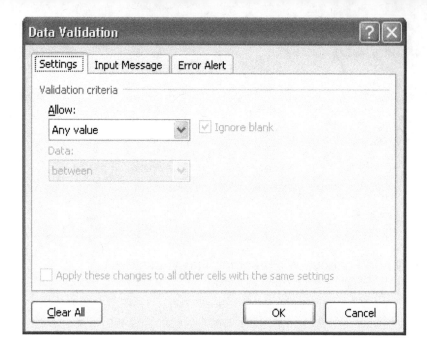

To create a drop-down list, click the down arrow just to the right of "Allow: Any Value" on the Settings tab:

Select List from the drop-down menu, and you'll see a new area appear:

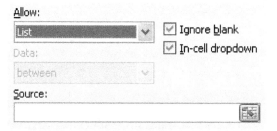

Select List from the drop-down menu, and you'll see a new area appear:

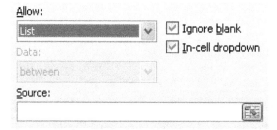

Source means which data you want to go in your list. You can either just type in your cell references here or let Excel do it for you.

To let Excel, handle the job, click the icon to the right of the Source textbox:

When you click this icon, the Data Validation dialogue box will shrink:

Now select the cells on your spreadsheet that you want in your list. For us, this is the Students.

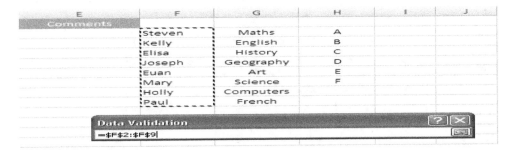

Once you have selected your data, click the same icon on the Data Validation dialogue box. You'll then be returned to the full size one, with your cell references filled in for you:

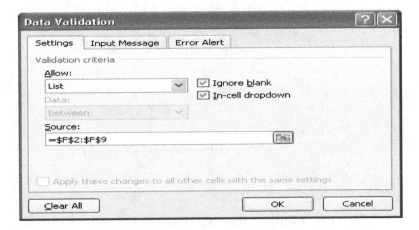

Click OK, and you'll see the A column with a drop-down list in cell A1:

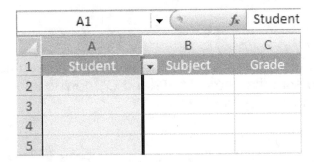

However, you don't want a drop-down list for your A1 column heading. To get rid of it, click inside of cell A1. Click the Data Validation item on the Data Tools panel again to bring up the dialogue box. From the Allow list, select Any Value:

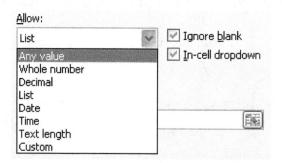

Click OK on the Data Validation dialogue box, and your drop-down list in cell A1 will be gone.
The rest of the column will still have drop down lists, though. Try it out. Click inside cell A2, and you'll see a down-pointing arrow:

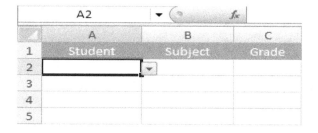

Click the arrow to see your list:

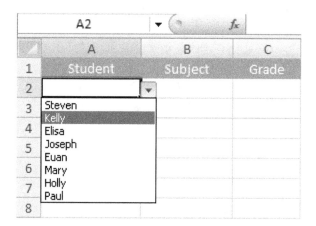

Select an item on your list to enter that name in the cell. Click any other cell in the A column and you'll see the same list.
Adding a drop-down list to your cell can save you a lot of time. And it means that typing errors won't creep into your work.

Exercise
Add drop down list to the B and C columns. The B column should contain lists of Subjects, and the C column a list of Grades. Make sure that the cells B1 and C1 don't contain drop down lists. When you're finished, the Subject column should look like this:

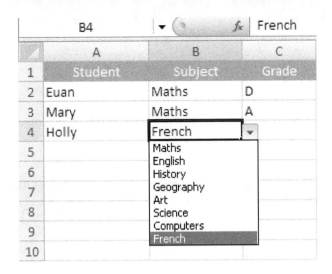

And the Grade column should look like this:

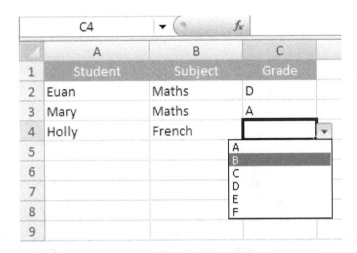

7.3 WEB INTEGRATION

A Web Query is when you send a request to a web page and ask for some data to be returned.

There are many reasons why you would want to do that. If, for example, you're a hard-working salesperson out in the field, and a customer wants the latest prices, you could run a web query in Excel and pull the prices from your employer's website.

How to run a Web Query in Excel

You'll now learn how to use Web Queries in Excel. For this lesson, you'll need an active internet connection. We're going to connect to a web page and download a product list straight into a spreadsheet. Off we go!

- Open Excel
- Connect to the internet if you're not already online.
- Click inside A1 on your new worksheet.
- From the Excel Ribbon, click on Data.
- From the Data tab, locate the Get and Transform Data panel:

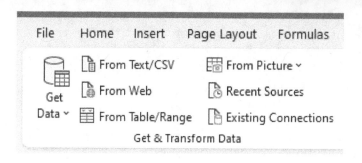

From the Get and Transform Data panel, click on From Web. You'll then see the following dialogue box appear:

The idea is that you type the address of a web page and then click Go. Excel will then fetch the data for you.
So, in the Address box, where it says about: blank in the image, type any address:
http:// www.google.com
Before you click ok. You'll see this dialogue box appear:

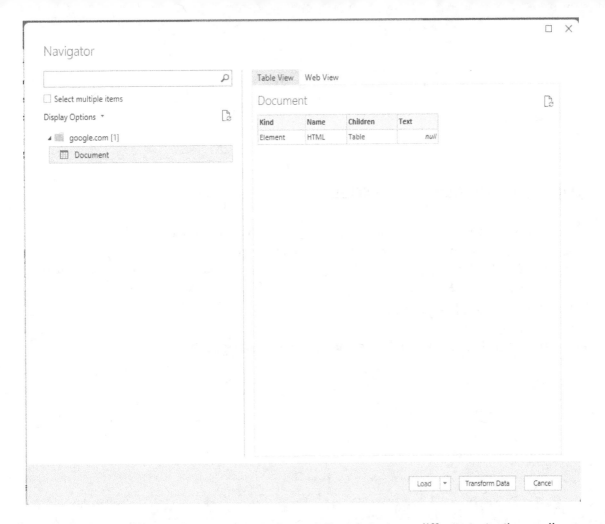

There's not much to do, here. But if you want to import the data to a different starting cell, or even a new worksheet, click Load To option. For this import, Excel is only giving us the option to view the data as a Table.

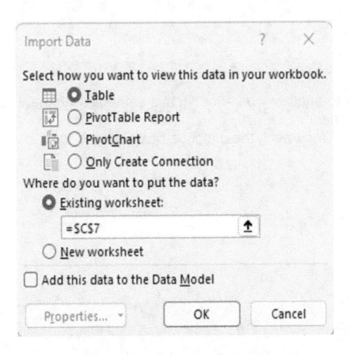

Click Transform Data and the import will begin. You should see this in cell A1 on your spreadsheet:

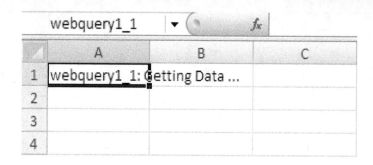

7.4 HOW TO INSERT HYPERLINKS IN EXCEL

You can place Hyperlinks in the cells on your spreadsheet. To quickly go to a different worksheet or workbook, you would simply click the link. We'll see how to do that now.

- Click inside of cell A1 of a new spreadsheet. From the Excel Ribbon, click the Insert tab.
- From the Insert tab, locate the Links panel.
- Click on Link and then Insert Link

When you click the insert link item, you'll see the following dialogue box appear:

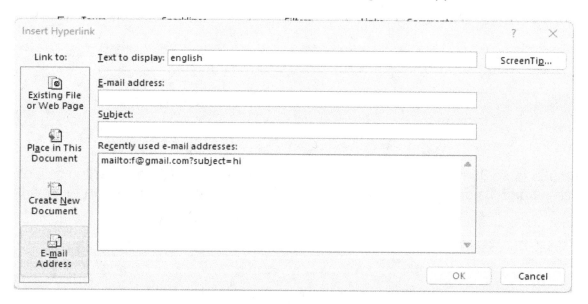

We're going to create a link to another worksheet in this same spreadsheet. So, under Link to on the left, click on "Place in This Document".

When you click Place in This Document, the dialogue box changes to this:

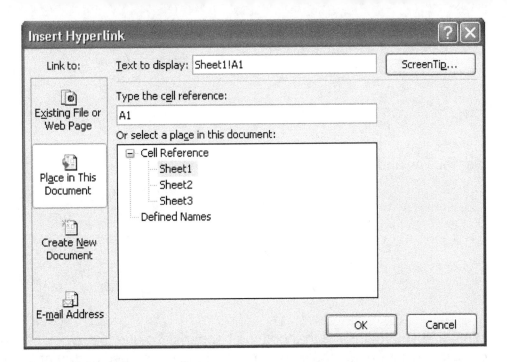

We'll try linking to Sheet3 on our spreadsheet. When the link is clicked on Sheet1, we want to jump to a specific cell on Sheet3.

- Under "Or select a place in this document", click on Sheet3.
- Type some text in the Text to display box at the top. This is the text of your hyperlink, as it will display in the cell.
- Click the Screen Tip button at the top and type some text for when the mouse is over the link.

Your dialogue box will then look something like this one:

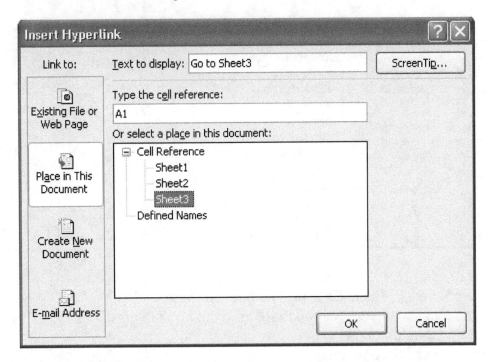

Click OK when you're done, and you'll see cell A1 on your spreadsheet change:

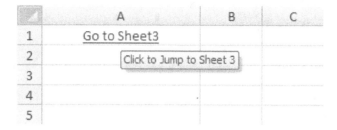

	A	B	C
1	Go to Sheet3		
2			
3			
4			
5			

Hold your mouse over the link and you should see your Screen Tip:

	A	B	C
1	Go to Sheet3		
2	Click to Jump to Sheet 3		
3			
4			
5			

Try to click on your link, and you might find that nothing happens! To use the hyperlink, you must click the link and hold your mouse down for a second or so. Let go of the left mouse button and you should jump to Sheet 3.

If you want to open an existing spreadsheet, instead of jumping to a location in the current one, click the Hyperlink item on the Links panel to bring up the dialogue box again.

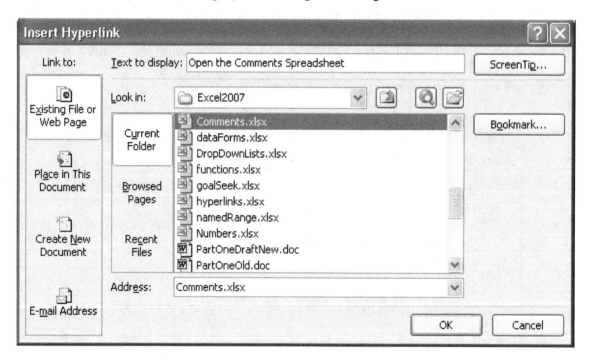

- Under Link to on the left, select Existing File or Web Page.
- Navigate to the location of your spreadsheet from the Look in area.
- Select the spreadsheet to open.
- Type some text, and a Screen tip.
- Then click OK.

When you click your new link, the spreadsheet file you selected will open.

But we'll leave this brief introduction to the subject of Web Integration in Excel. There's a whole lot more you can do in this area: Upload your spreadsheet data to the web, instead of downloading like we did; save your spreadsheet as a web page; create a spreadsheet that others can interact with, email your spreadsheets, and a whole lot more besides.

7.5 INSERT DRAWING OBJECTS INTO YOUR EXCEL SPREADSHEETS

A drawing can liven up a dull spreadsheet. Some good line art, or even simple shapes, can help illustrate your data. In this lesson, you'll see how to add simple shapes, and textboxes to your spreadsheet.
First, look at the spreadsheet below. Unless you know about Cosines, Adjacent angles, and Hypotenuse, the data below will be a bit bewildering:

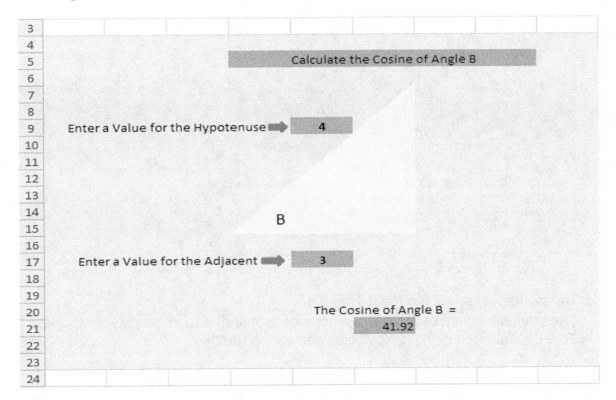

However, add a few shapes, along with some color, and it becomes clearer what the data is for (the Cosine in the image below has been formatted to 2 decimal places):

We'll now show you how to produce a spreadsheet like the one above. Don't worry if you haven't a clue about Cosines - it's not important for this lesson. (We'll show you the formula, though.)

7.6 HOW TO DRAW A SHAPE ON AN EXCEL SPREADSHEET

To insert a shape on your spreadsheet, do the following.

- From the Excel Ribbon, click on Insert.
- Locate the Shapes panel:

On the Shapes panel, click the drop-down arrow to see all the available shapes:

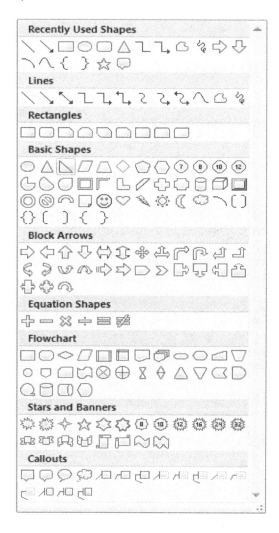

- Under Basic Shapes, select the Right Triangle
- Hold down your left mouse button on your spreadsheet and drag to create your shape. Let go when you have a decent sized triangle. You'll see something like this:

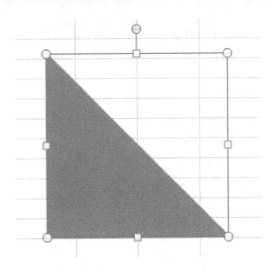

The green circle allows you to rotate the shape. The other circles (and squares) are sizing handles. Hold your mouse down over one of these and drag to resize your shape, if it's not the size you want it.

But we'd like the triangle pointing the other way. So, hold your mouse down on the green circle, and drag to rotate your triangle:

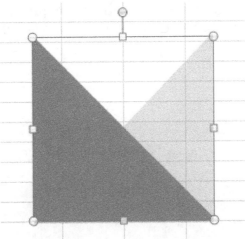

You should see an outline, like the one above. Let go of your left mouse button when it is in position:

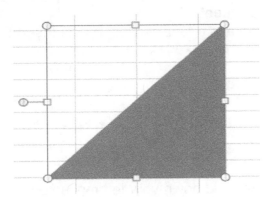

As you can see, the green circle is now on the left-hand side.

If you look on the Excel Ribbon at the top, you'll notice that it has changed - a Format tab has appeared. You'll see all the various options for shapes. Locate Shape Fill on the Shape Styles panel, and click to see the Fill options:

231

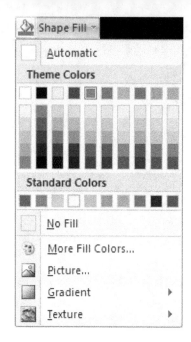

Select a color for your triangle. You'll also want to select a Shape Outline, underneath Shape Fill. Select the same color as your Fill, and your triangle will look something like this one:

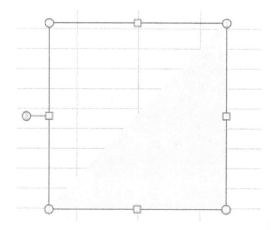

Add a Text Box to an Excel Spreadsheet
To get the letter B in the triangle, we'll add a text box. So, on the Insert Shapes panel again, you'll notice a Text Box option. Click on this to select it:

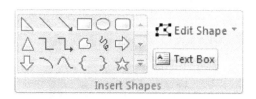

Now move back to your spreadsheet, hold down your left mouse button, and drag out a Text Box. Let go of the left mouse button and you'll have something like this:

With the cursor inside of the Text Box, simply type the letter B. Because it's text, you can highlight your letter and format it. In the image below, we've increased the font size.

We now need to drag our Text Box onto the shape. Move your mouse over the Text Box until the cursor changes shape to four arrowheads (this can be tricky):

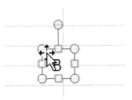

Once your cursor changes shape, hold down the left mouse button and drag your Text Box on to the triangle:

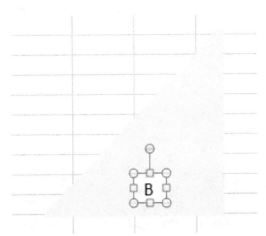

With the Text Box selected, use the arrow keys on your keyboard to nudge it into position. Fill the Text Box in the same way as you did for the triangle. To get rid of the text box border, click Shape Outline just below Shape Fill. Set it to No Outline. It will then look like this:

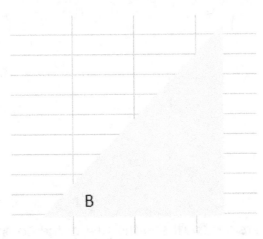

If you need to move your triangle and Text Box, you can select them both at the same time, and drag them as one. Click on your Triangle to select it. Now hold down the CTRL key on your keyboard. With the CTRL key held down, click on your Text Box. Both will now be selected:

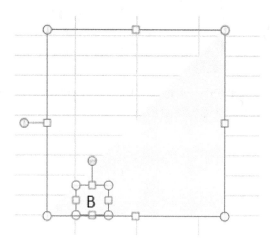

With both the triangle and the Text Box selected, hold your mouse over the selected shapes. When your cursor changes to the four arrowheads, hold down the left button and drag your shapes to a new position:

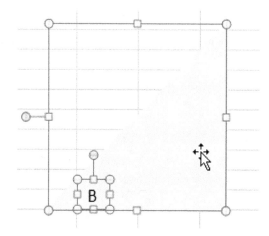

You can finish off the formatting in the normal way. In the image below, we selected all the cells surrounding the shape, and added a background color from the Home menu, Font panel.

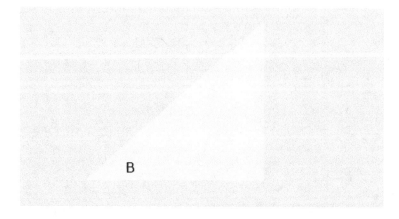

If you look again at the finished version, you'll see the rest of the colors we chose. These are just filled cells from the Home > Font panel:

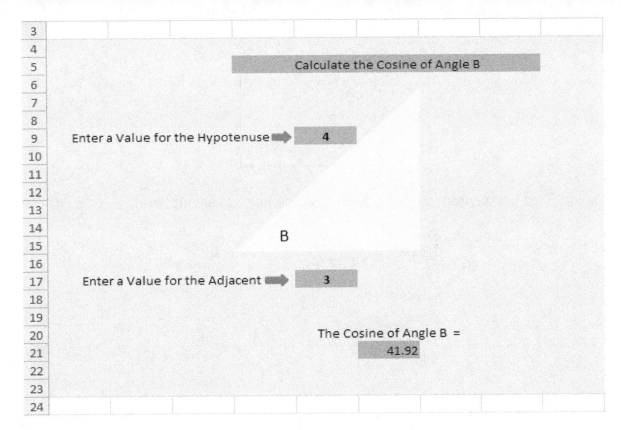

The text in the cells is just entered in the normal way. The formula for the Cosine in cell G22 of our spreadsheet has this syntax:

=DEGREES(COS(Adjacent_Cell_Reference / Hypotenuse_ Cell_Reference))

An example of how to use is it this:

=DEGREES(COS(F18 / F10))

When the user types in a value for the Hypotenuse or the Adjacent, the Cosine number will change.

But you can add any shapes you want to liven up your spreadsheet. It doesn't have to look plain, white, and dull!

7.7 HOW TO ADD AN ERROR MESSAGE TO AN EXCEL SPREADSHEET

In the previous part, you saw how to add drop down lists to your Excel spreadsheets. In this part, we'll display an error message for our users. If you haven't already done so, you need to do the previous tutorial first.

Data Validation - restricting what data can go in a cell.

You can also restrict what goes into a cell on your spreadsheet and display an error message for your users. We'll do this with our Comments column. If users enter too much text, we'll let them know by displaying a suitable error box. Try the following:

- Highlight the E column on your spreadsheet (the Comments column)
- From the Data Tools panel, click Data Validation to bring up the dialogue box again.
- From the Allow list, select Text length:

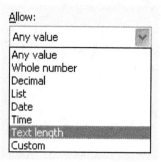

When you select Text Length from the list, you'll see three new areas appear:

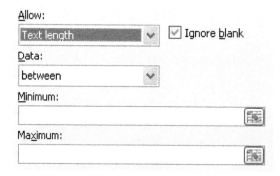

What we're trying to do is to restrict the amount of text a user can input into any one cell on the Comments column. We'll restrict the text to between 0 and 25 characters.

The first of the new areas (Data) is exactly what we want - Between. For the minimum textbox, just type a 0 (zero) in there. For the maximum box, type 25. Your dialogue box should then look like this:

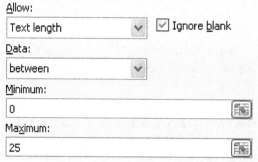

To add an error message, click the Error Alert tab at the top of the Data Validation dialogue box:

Make sure there is a tick in the box for "Show error alert after invalid data is entered".
You have three different Styles to choose from for your error message. Click the drop-down list to see them:

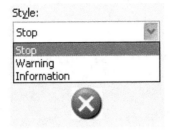

In the Title textbox, type some text for the title of your error message.

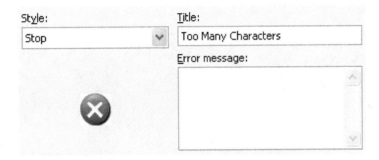

Now click inside the error message field and type some text for the main body of your error message. This will tell the user what he or she did wrong:

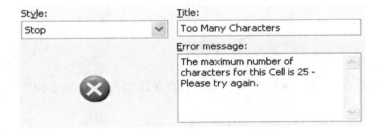

Click OK on the Data Validation dialogue box when you're done.
To test out your new error message, click inside any cell in your Comments Column. Type a message longer than 25 characters. Press the enter key on your keyboard and you should see your error message appear:

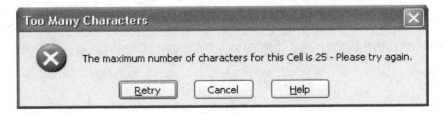

As you can see, the user is prompted to Retry or Cancel. But our title (Too many characters) is at the top, our Stop symbol is to the left, and our Error message is displaying nicely!

7.8 HIDING SPREADSHEET DATA IN EXCEL

The data that went into our lists doesn't need to be on show for all to see. You can hide this text quite easily.

- Highlight the columns with your data in it (F, G and H for us)
- Click on the Home tab from the top of Excel.
- Locate the Cells panel.
- On the Cells panel, click on Format. You'll see the following menu:

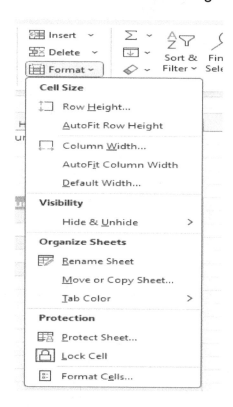

Move your mouse down to Hide & Unhide and you'll see a Sub Menu appear:

Click on Hide Columns from the Sub menu. Excel will hide the columns you selected:

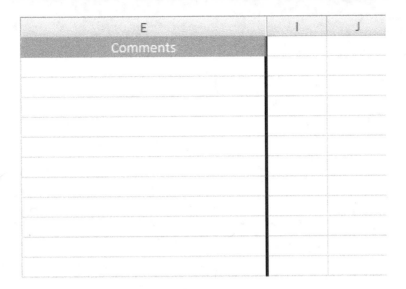

In the spreadsheet above, the columns F to H are no longer visible.
To get them back again, highlight the columns E and I. From the same sub menu, click Unhide Columns.

HOW TO INSERT AN EXCEL SPREADSHEET INTO A MICROSOFT WORD DOCUMENT

Spreadsheets are inserted into Word documents using something called Object Linking and Embedding. Object Linking and Embedding (or OLE), can be a complicated subject, but basically, it's used when you want to insert something from one program into another program. The example you're going to see will embed a spreadsheet chart into Microsoft Word.
You have two choices when you want to embed something from Excel into another program - to use linking or embedding. If you use linking, you can update the data in Excel and see the changes in the other program; if you use embedding, any changes you make to Excel will not show up in the other program.
First, here's how to create a Linked Object. The two-program used will be Excel and Word. So, if you have Microsoft Word and Excel, open both programs.
In Excel, create the following spreadsheet:

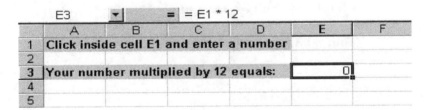

All the spreadsheet does is multiply whatever is in cell E1 by 12. The answer goes in cell E3. (This example is not terribly functional: you wouldn't really want to use OLE with this spreadsheet. But it's easy to create and will serve as an example of how to use Linking.)
- Once you have created your spreadsheet, highlight from A1 to E3
- With your data highlighted, click on Edit form the menu bar.
- From the drop-down menu, click on Copy.
- Switch to Microsoft Word.
- In Microsoft Word, click on Edit from the menu bar.
- From the drop-down menu, click on Paste Special
- A dialogue box pops up in Word like the one below:

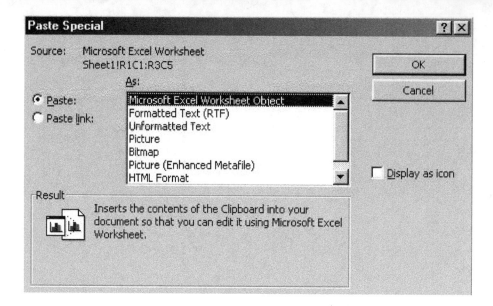

- In the main list box, click on Microsoft Excel Worksheet Object
- Of the two Option buttons on the left, Paste and Paste Link, choose Paste Link by clicking on it.
- Click the OK button at the top.

Word now goes to work and embeds your spreadsheet into the Word-processed document. Because we chose Paste Link, we will be able to view any updates made from Excel. The Word document should look like the one below:

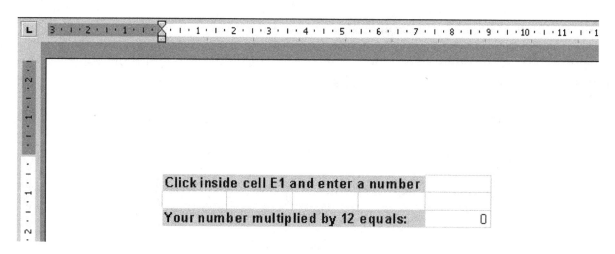

To see that it really does update in Word, do this:

- Go back to your Excel spreadsheet.
- Click inside cell E1.
- Type in the number 7
- Press the Return key on your keyboard.
- The number 84 should appear in cell E3.
- Switch back to Microsoft Word and view the results.
- The Word document will now look like this.

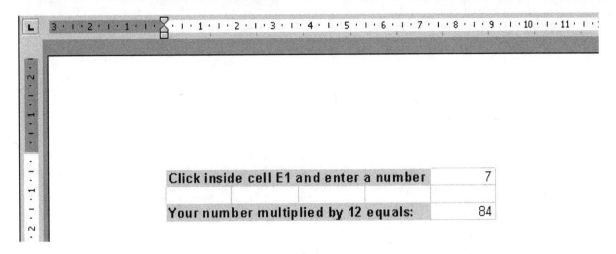

Click inside cell E1 and enter a number				7
Your number multiplied by 12 equals:				84

As you can see, the numbers from the Excel spreadsheet are now in the Word document. The link worked!

If you don't want Word updating the embedded object, you would select Paste instead of Paste Link from the Paste Special dialogue box. Everything else is the same.

Things like Charts and Pivot Tables are the ones usually embedded into a Word document, all ready for the company presentation.

7.9 ANALYSE DATA WITH ANALYSIS TOOLPAK

Excel has an add-on called "Analysis ToolPak", which can perform a statistical analysis of a quantity of data. Analysis ToolPak is an add-on that is not installed initially, so it must be loaded before you can use it.

INSTALLATION OF ANALYSIS TOOLPAK

To install Analysis Toolpak , do the following:
1. Click on the File tab on top left on the screen.
2. Click on the Excel Option button.
3. In the left side of the window that opens, click on Get Add-Ins.
4. Select Analysis Toolpak from the list of add-ins.
5. At the bottom of the window, make sure that by "Manage" there is Excel Add-Ins
6. Click on the Finish button.
7. In the box that opens, ensure there is a" check" mark next to Analysis Toolpak.
8. Click on OK.
During this procedure, the program might require the installation of something from the installation disk, which you should just go ahead and do.

A QUICK ANALYSIS WITH ANALYSIS TOOLPAK

In Figure below, there are some numbers which we will use for a small analysis

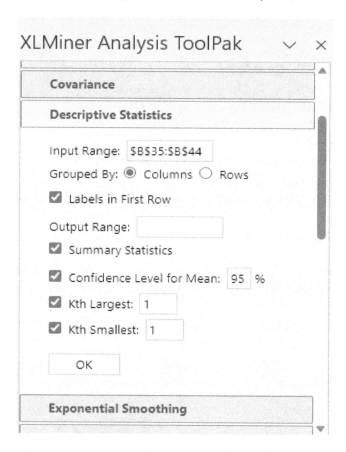

	A	B	C
34			
35		12	
36		13	
37		42	
38		45	
39		34	
40		45	
41		54	
42		65	
43		67	
44		23	
45			

1. Make a list like the one in Figure above.
2. Click on the Data Tab in the Ribbon.
3. Click on the Data Analysis button, which is located furthest to the right in the Ribbon if you have installed Analysis Toolpak.
4. A window opens with a list of tools for analysis. Choose Descriptive Statistics and click OK.

XLMiner Analysis ToolPak ∨ ✕

Covariance

Descriptive Statistics

Input Range: $B$35:$B$44

Grouped By: ◉ Columns ○ Rows

☑ Labels in First Row

Output Range:

☑ Summary Statistics

☑ Confidence Level for Mean: 95 %

☑ Kth Largest: 1

☑ Kth Smallest: 1

OK

Exponential Smoothing

5. A new window opens, where you must specify several settings. Set the settings as shown in Figure above.
6. Click OK.

A new Tab is added to the workbook.
It is called "Score" and contains the results of the analysis.
If you frequently need to perform a statistical analysis on a volume of data, the Analysis ToolPak in many cases can save you a lot of time.

	A	B
	B3	41
1	Collum 1	
2		
3	Avarage value	41
4	Standart Error	5,7658
5	Median	43,5
6	Condition	23
7	Standard Submission	18,23306
8	Sample variance	332,4444
9	Kurtosis	-0,90814
10	Varpage	-0,06118
11	Area	55
12	Minimum	12
13	Maximum	67
14	Sum	410
15	Number	10
16	Largest (1)	67
17	Smallest (1)	12
18	Confidence level	13,04314
19		

PART EIGHT:

PRINTING WITH EXCEL

8.1 VIEWING AND PRINTING

Viewing and printing is perhaps not so important compared to learning how to do spreadsheets, but when you start working more seriously with it, you will discover that there are some possibilities that are good to know about.

Printing Of course, you can print your spreadsheets, but often you will find that it requires a little adjustment and alignment before you get a satisfactory result.

It is not something that should cost you sleep at night, because when you have learned a few tricks, it is not a problem.

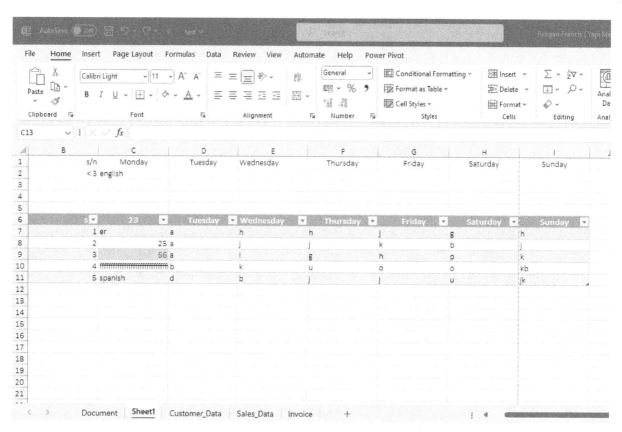

In Figure above there is an example of a table that takes up a lot of space. If you like, you can create a similar table, so you can practice yourself.

Content is not so important if you have roughly the same number of rows and columns as in the example.

PRINT PREVIEW

I always use the "Print Preview" function before I print. "Print Preview" shows what the printout will look like when it is sent to the printer.

1.Click on the File tab, point to the menu item Print, then click on Print.

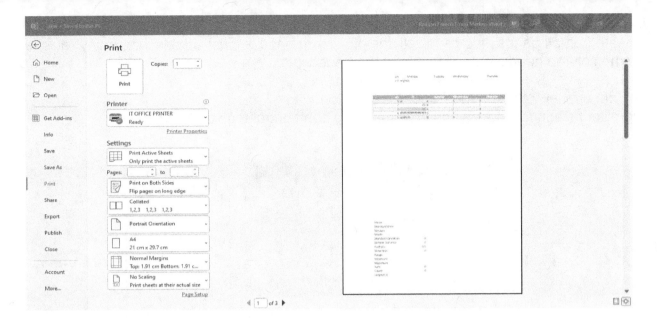

Now you will see an image of how the print will look with the current settings.

In our example in Figure below, the transcript is not optimal. The table in the spreadsheet has 13 columns, but only seven of them are displayed.

If you scroll down with your mouse, you get to page 3 where the rest of the table is displayed.

s/n	Monday	Tuesday	Wednesday	Thursday	Fri
< 3	english				

s/n	23	Tuesday	Wednesday	Thursday	Fri
1	er	a	h	h	j
2	25	s	j	j	k
3	56	a	i	g	h
4	ffff ffff ffff ffff ffff ffff	b	k	u	o
5	spanish	d	b	j	j

1 of 3

PAGE SETUP

We need to change some settings. Fortunately, you can adjust a lot of different things.

For instance, you can scale down. The content of the spreadsheet must be scaled down so that it fits on one page.

You can also adjust the margins and add headers and footers, which are text elements that appear at the top and bottom of each page of the transcript.

Finally, you can also set the number of rows and columns.
to be repeated on all pages. It is especially helpful if you need to print a table with many rows, since you can view the column headers on all pages of the transcript.

2. In the Print preview, click on the Page Setup button.
The "Page Setup" window opens and from here you can control the various options.

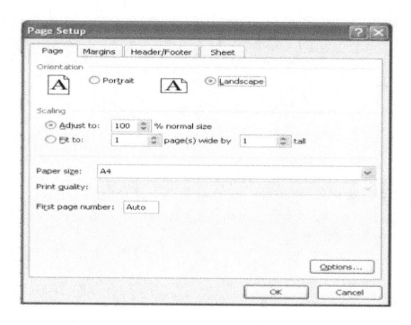

The window is divided into four different tabs called "Page", "Margins", "Header / Footer" and "Sheet". In the "Page" Tab you can choose the orientation, ie. choose between portrait and landscape paper format. You can also select the scaling of the content. The default scaling is 100%, but you can adjust it up and down manually until you get an outcome that suits you.

3.In this exercise, let Excel find an appropriate scaling by simply indicating that Excel must adapt the content in width and height to a specified number of pages in landscape format.

In our case we will probably get a suitable result by selecting one page wide by one page in height landscape format.

It is not always enough to scale the pages to get an appropriate result. Sometimes you need to precisely define where the page breaks should be. You will learn that in the next section on" viewing".

The "Margins" Tab in the "Page Setup" window is. Of course, you can set how big the margins should be in centimeters. This can also be done in another way. If you close the window "Page Setup" and set a marker at the display margins on the tape, you can adjust the margins visually using the mouse. I think this is easier to work with. The "Header / Footer" Tab allows you to display a fixed text at the top and bottom of each page of the transcript. This text could be company name, author, etc. But you can also add some text fields which automatically show the date, page number and filename.

The "Sheet" Tab is used to set what must be printed. You do not always want to print everything, and it may be necessary to repeat some rows or columns on all pages. Most settings in this Tab are not available if you opened the window "Page Setup" from within "Print Preview."

VIEWING

So far, our exercises have taken place in "Normal View". This is the standard way to display spreadsheets, and it is nicer when you work in the spreadsheet.

But there are a few other useful views you can use before you print your sheet. If you have a large spreadsheet you need to print, the result may well be somewhat disappointing because spreadsheets tend to spread out over several pages.

In the section on printing, you learned that you could scale the printout to fit into a specific number of pages, but you also could control exactly where the page breaks should be. The display buttons are located at the bottom right on the screen. You can get to the same features by clicking on the View Tab in the Ribbon, but the display buttons at the bottom are always visible, allowing you can save a mouse click. The display buttons consist of three buttons and a "zoom slider". The "zoom slider" works by clicking the mouse and dragging to the right or left to zoom in and out respectively.

I prefer instead to hold down the CTRL key on the keyboard while I scroll up or down with the scroll wheel on the mouse. It is a much easier way to zoom in and out, in my opinion, and this method can also be used in many Windows programs.

The other three view buttons switch between Normal, Page Layout and Show Page Breaks. We are already familiar with Normal, since it is the view, we have been using in all our exercises so far. This is the best view when you just must work with the spreadsheet without caring about the print layout.

Page Layout shows something like the result if you print out the spreadsheet.

Show Page Breaks are the most useful alternative view since it also adds an important functionality.

Here you can see and adjust what should and should not be printed. You can insert and rearrange page breaks and exclude certain areas from being printed.

ADJUST PRINT RANGE

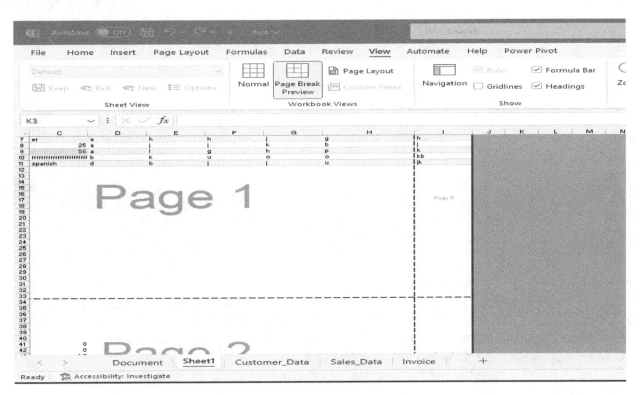

1. Click on the Show Page Break button to display the same screen as in Figure above.

In the example in Figure above, I have changed the page setup from the previous exercise, so the scaling is 100% again.

Page layout is still landscape format. The repetition of the first row and column has also been disabled.

The table is surrounded by a thick blue border, which defines "printable area". Only those cells that are in the frame will be printed.

You can, by pointing to the frame with your mouse and holding the left mouse button, move the frame.

That way you can also exclude some of the table for printing, if that is what you want.

You can also have several separate areas in the spreadsheet as a part of the print area.

To illustrate this, it requires that our example be extended with a Couple of extra tables.

2. Click on the view button Normal and add a few tables like the ones shown in Figure below.

Also add some text in some other cells that you do not want printed.

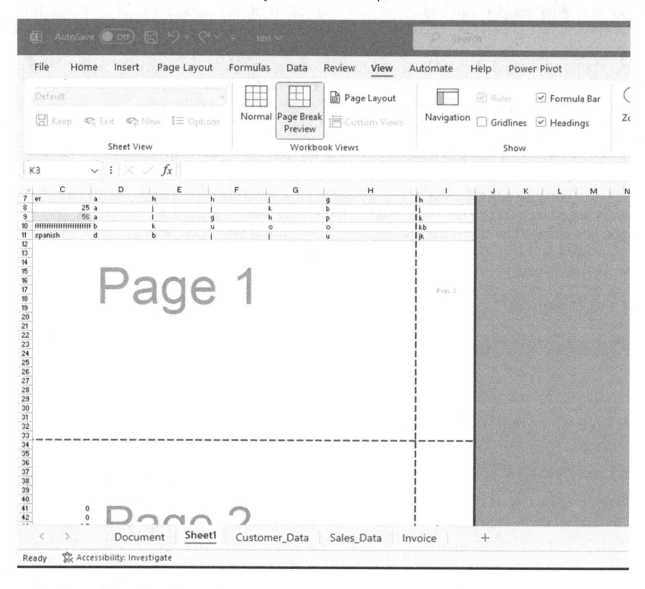

3. Change to Show Page Breaks again.

You can still see that the original table is inside the white area, which means that it will be printed.

But the new tables are outside the printable area and will therefore not be printed If you have several different areas in the same spreadsheet that you want printed, you can hold down the CTRL key on your keyboard while you select the different areas with the mouse.

When you are finished selecting fields, click the right mouse button on one of the areas and select the menu item Set Print Area:

4. Hold down the CTRL key while you select all three tables with the mouse. Do not select that which you do not want to print.

5. Right-click on any of the highlighted areas and click the menu item Set Print Area.

We now have a "composite print area" and the spreadsheet will look like Figure below.

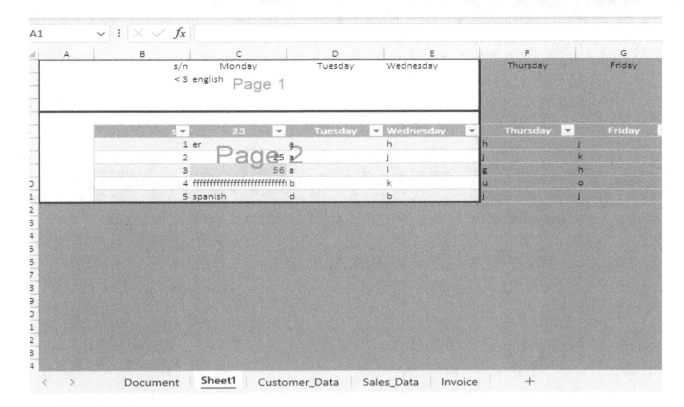

MANAGING PAGE BREAKS

In our exercise, there is an automatic page break down through the multiplication table.
It is signified by a dotted blue line.
Excel decides where the automatic page breaks should be, and your spreadsheet might show something else.
It depends on the cell heights and column widths, but it also depends on your printer and its configuration.
To gain more control over where the page breaks are, you can insert permanent page breaks. Fixed page breaks will not move, and if you put them in the right places, you can avoid unfortunate automatic page breaks.
Insertion of fixed page breaks is always on the left and above the cell which is active.
Our multiplication table in the example would obviously spread out over two pages. In my spreadsheet the table was divided by an automatic page break between the columns for October and November.
I would like the shift to be between Wednesday and Thursday, so I make H1 the active cell.

1. In your spreadsheet, activate the cell, where it says "Wednesday".
2. Make sure the Page Layout Tab in the Ribbon is selected and click on the Shift button.
3. In the menu that appears, click on Insert Page Break.

The shift buttons.
Now there are no automatic page breaks, and there will not be any unless you make the sheet bigger.

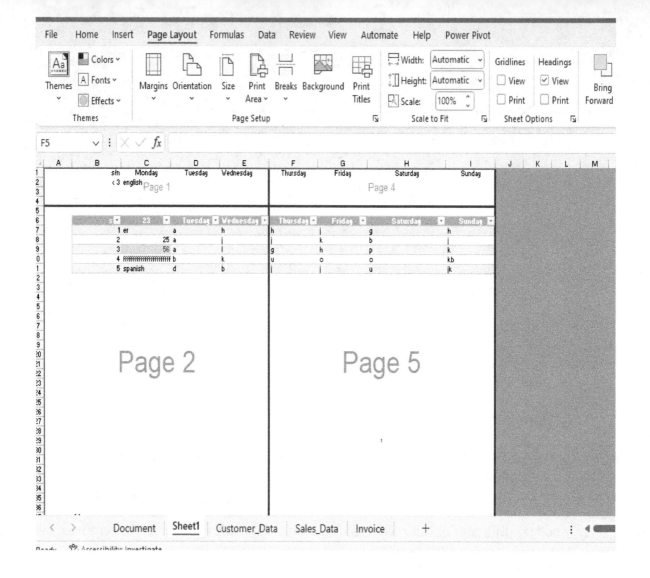

s/n	Monday	Tuesday	Wednesday	Thursday	Friday	Saturday	Sunday